The Power of Meditation and Prayer

QUOTES ABOUT MICHAEL TOMS

"...one of the best interviewers who has ever worked the American airwaves, radio, or TV."

— Robert Fuller, physicist, educator, past
president of Oberlin College, and active
citizen diplomat

"Someone with whom I have cruised some important realms of the cosmic ocean and in doing so have developed ever-increasing confidence in his intuitive navigation."

— R. Buckminster Fuller (1895–1983),
inventor of the geodesic dome; designer,
philosopher, and creator of the World Games

"...Bill Moyers and Michael Toms are alike: two of the most creative interviewers it has been my good fortune to work with."

— Joseph Campbell (1904–1987), mythologist
and author of *Hero with a Thousand Faces,
The Masks of God, Myths to Live By,* and
The Mythic Image

Please visit the Hay House Website at:
www.hayhouse.com

and the New Dimensions Website at:
www.newdimensions.org

THE POWER
OF MEDITATION
AND PRAYER

LARRY DOSSEY, M.D., JON KABAT-ZINN,
SOGYAL RINPOCHE, JACK KORNFIELD,
MARSHA SINETAR, SHINZEN YOUNG,
JEANNE ACHTERBERG, GAY HENDRICKS,
NEALE DONALD WALSCH AND
FR. BEDE GRIFFITHS

WITH MICHAEL TOMS

HAY HOUSE, INC.
CARLSBAD, CA

Copyright © 1997 by New Dimensions Foundation

Published and distributed in the United States by:
Hay House, Inc., P.O. Box 5100, Carlsbad, CA 92018-5100 • (800) 654-5126
(800) 650-5115 (fax)

Edited by Michael Toms, Rose Holland, and the Hay House editorial staff
Introduction, Prologues, and Epilogues by Michael Toms
Designed by Jenny Richards

Library of Congress Cataloging-in-Publication Data

Dossey, Larry, 1940–
    The power of meditation and prayer / Larry Dossey, and other
contributors; with Michael Toms.
        p.   cm.
    ISBN 1-56170-423-7 (trade paper)
    1. Meditation. 2. Prayer. 3. Spiritual life. I. Toms, Michael.
II. Title.
BL627.D67   1997
291.4'3—dc21   97-11492
                                          CIP

ISBN 1-56170-423-7

00 99 98 97   4 3 2 1
First Printing, September 1997

Printed in the United States of America

CONTENTS

☙ ☙ ☙

Editor's note: Throughout the book, the interviewer's
questions are in italics.

PREFACE

About New Dimensions

New Dimensions Radio is the major activity of the New Dimensions Foundation, a nonprofit educational organization. "New Dimensions" is an international radio interview series featuring thousands of hours of in-depth dialogues on a wide variety of topics. **Michael Toms,** the co-founder of New Dimensions Radio, the award-winning host of the "New Dimensions" radio interview series—and a widely respected New Paradigm spokesperson and scholar himself—engages in thoughtful, intimate conversations with the leading thinkers and social innovators of our time, focusing on creative and positive approaches to the challenges of a changing society.

About This Book

Prayer and meditation are available to all of us. This book provides an expansive view of the nature of the process from several different perspectives. Remembering that each of us prays in our own unique way, it is still useful to listen to what others can tell us, especially those with experience. There is considerable wisdom within these pages, and it remains for each of us to read, reflect, and take away whatever we resonate with, and integrate it into our own practice.

There are no "shoulds" for praying or meditating other than being open and receptive. In a profound way, both involve letting go of whatever we're holding on to and simply allowing life to unfold. So, I invite you to let go into this book, apply what works for you, and discard what doesn't. Listen for that still, small voice within, honor it, and follow your own path.

INTRODUCTION

This book is about learning to live your life as a meditation or prayer. Most of us were taught that we should pray at certain times or in certain places. Many of the meditative practices that have come to the West during the second half of the 20th century have emphasized the monastic or retreat aspect of meditation. Other cultural traditions demonstrate that the sacred can be integrated into the dailiness of life, where every activity becomes a prayer offering or a meditative act. The Balinese are such an example with their daily offerings, ritual dancing, reverence for nature, and sacred art.

You will discover through the dialogues included here that it is possible, indeed, desirable, to integrate prayer and/or meditation into your daily life. The news of prayer's power to heal that Dr. Larry Dossey provides in the first chapter would be in headlines across the nation if it were a pill. Jon Kabat-Zinn reminds us of the importance of paying attention each moment, and becoming more awake and aware. Sogyal Rinpoche brings the wisdom of a millennia-old spiritual tradition to bear on the challenge of contemporary life in a material world. Insight meditation teacher Jack Kornfield reveals some of the pitfalls and challenges of the spiritual path, while providing some profound insights about meditation practice, especially for Westerners. Marsha Sinetar, a practicing contemplative herself, tells about her own experience in working with silence and solitude. Her practical wisdom can be beneficially applied by anyone on the spiritual quest.

Meditation master Shinzen Young presents a grounded and useful approach to contemplative practice, again one that has been tempered through the fires of real life experience, not philosophical theory. The power of the imagination, an integral and important aspect of both prayer and meditation during certain stages, is the central focus of Jeanne Achterberg's remarks. Gay Hendricks brings us back to the basics of breathing and why the breath is not only crucial to life itself, but how learning to breathe is an essential component in unifying mind, body, and spirit. Interesting revelations emerge that will furnish food for thoughtful reflection during the dialogue with Neale Donald Walsch, as he candidly talks about his engaging God in conversation. The final contributor, the late Father Bede Griffiths, speaks to the soul in all of us, and in his gentle way he reminds us of what is truly important in order to live a spiritual life.

The key to this book is that each of the chapters is part of a larger whole, and each of the individual perspectives is interrelated with one another. The complete tapestry of what all of the contributors have to tell us underscores the title of the book. Our wish is that you, the reader, will find these dialogues useful and relevant for your own spiritual practice, whatever it may be.

—Michael Toms
Ukiah, California
June 1997

CHAPTER ONE

MEDICINE, MEANING, AND PRAYER

Larry Dossey, M.D., with Michael Toms

PROLOGUE

*W*e *know from a* Newsweek *cover story on prayer that 91 percent of all women pray, as do 85 percent of men. Indeed, more of us will pray than will go to work, exercise, or have sexual relations. There is an abundance of scientific studies published in journals supporting the efficacy of prayer. Mostly unread by physicians, as well as patients, even clergy and deeply religious people are uninformed about this bonanza of information. It is no longer a matter of faith. The facts are that prayer works to heal. Prayer actually heals. In this chapter, we will explore the power of prayer and what the healing process is all about.*

Larry Dossey lectures internationally and in 1988 was invited to deliver the annual Mahatma Gandhi Memorial Lecture in New Delhi, India. He is the only physician ever invited to do so. Larry is the former Chief of Staff of Humana Medical City Dallas Hospital in Dallas, Texas, and the former Co-Chairman of the panel on Mind/Body Interventions, Office of Alternative Medicine of the National Institutes of Health. He is also the author of seven books, including Meaning and Medicine; Healing Words: The Power of Prayer and the Practice of Medicine; *and* Prayer Is Good Medicine. *He is executive editor of* Alternative Therapies in Health and Medicine.

MICHAEL TOMS: *Larry, do you have a simple definition of prayer? Is there one?*

LARRY DOSSEY: Probably not. I was astonished while researching this whole area, going through dozens and dozens of books written by world-class authorities on prayer, that often there was not a single definition offered on what the subject of the book was. This is quite an oddity. I think most people in this culture grow up thinking that prayer is talking to a male cosmic parent figure who basically prefers being addressed in English. I want to draw the canvas a lot wider, though, and define prayer in a different way. For me, prayer is any act that brings one in closer contact with the transcendent. It may involve words, but more often than not, it involves silence and privacy.

I don't think prayer necessarily even involves the awake, aware state. I'm convinced that prayer can be deeply unconscious. There are some fabulous stories that have to do with healing events wherein people pray in their dreams. So prayer is a very complex way of communicating with something outside of ourselves. But we don't want to lock ourselves into a very narrow definition of prayer at the outset, in which we say that it necessarily has to do with words. Because I'm convinced it doesn't.

Prayer is not usually something that one associates with the traditional healing or health establishment. Most hospitals aren't run by a religious order. There's not any intention or emphasis placed on prayer. Why is that, if prayer is so good?

Prayer is an embarrassment to the medical profession. I don't know any nicer way to put it. We can't acknowledge that it has any substance for one primary reason: There's no theory in modern medical science that explains how it could even be true. So lacking a theory, most physicians feel compelled to say that it doesn't work. This really loads the dice against looking at any empirical evidence. You know ahead of time that it must be flawed, so you can't stand up publicly in favor of prayer if you're a bona fide physician and value yourself as a scientifically inclined person. You just can't do that, and that's why I think you see it being marginalized in healing institutions.

So you don't learn about prayer in medical school?

As far as I recall, it was never even mentioned during all of my training.

So one of the contributions of the book Healing Words *is that you've uncovered a lot of what has to be called scientifically valid research on the power of prayer.*

These studies frankly knocked my socks off. I didn't get into this area voluntarily. I feel like I was basically dragged, kicking and screaming, into it for one basic reason: I value science. I consider myself to be sort of a science junkie, and these studies, which I stumbled onto, really shook me up. It led to questions like: You claim to be a scientifically oriented person; what are you going to do with this information? Are you going to honor it? Are you going to let it make a difference in the way you practice medicine? I think that the job of a medical scientist is to go through the data—wherever it may take you and whatever violence it may do to your preconceived ideas about how the world ought to work. If you have to revise those ideas, then so much for those ideas. I was reasonably shaken up by the discovery of this data.

The thing, I think, that sets the book *Healing Words* apart from most of the books that have been written on prayer is that practically none of them even acknowledged the existence of these controlled, prospective, randomized clinical studies—these laboratory studies that have been done under exotic fulfillment of stringent laboratory scientific criteria. So the information is out there, and my challenge to my colleagues is to say: Here's the information. Let's play science, and let's honor all the data. This data is not going to go away; it's here to be dealt with.

What are some of the more striking experiments?

The one that probably historically will come to be regarded as the study of the century—I suspect that it started this whole reassessment of scientific prayer—is the study that was done in San Francisco General Hospital back in 1988 by a cardiologist on the staff of UC San Francisco Medical School, Randolph Byrd. Dr. Byrd studied 393 patients, all of whom were admitted to the coronary care unit, basically with heart attacks or severe chest pain. They all got state-of-the-art coronary care, but half of these people were prayed for, and this was a double-blind study. The doctors, nurses, and patients didn't know who was and who wasn't being prayed for. Basically, in this study, it appeared as if the prayed-for patients had been slipped some sort of miracle drug. There were fewer deaths in the prayed-for group. Nobody in the prayed-for group wound up on the mechanical ventilator being artificially breathed for, while 12 in the unprayed-for group had to have that done. There were other areas of statistical significance in how these two groups did.

I must say, if what was being evaluated in that study had not been prayer, but a new medication, this would have been called a modern medical breakthrough. This is one study involving humans. Most of the studies—and I'm happy to be able to say this—do not involve humans. They involve lower-life forms such as bacteria, yeast, fungi, germinating seeds, mice, rats, ducks, and baby gerbils. People have experimented on the oddest creatures with prayer. It's important that it was done this way, since one of the criticisms that's always leveled at these prayer experiments on humans is that somehow the people knew that they were being prayed for, so what you see is just the effects of suggestion and placebo responses. You can't make that kind of complaint, though, against bacteria. Presumably they don't know they've been prayed for, and are not subject to the effects of suggestion or the placebo response.

So, you get around a lot of the perennial criticism of prayer research in humans by doing these studies on so-called lower life-forms. In over half of these studies, you see statistical significance, meaning that you can't ascribe the effects to chance. These studies have been performed at medical schools, universities, and independent research centers. They've been the subject of Ph.D. dissertations, master's theses, and so on. There really is a ton of data out there, and it's not commonly known.

If you can't make prayer into a pill, and you can't put it in a bottle or wrap it into a package, then it does come up against the scientific worldview that you have to see it, touch it, feel it, smell it, manipulate it, and turn it around. You can't do that with prayer, because it doesn't fit the accepted norms.

In a nutshell, there are all sorts of financial dis-incentives against using prayer as therapeutic intervention. I imagine that if some pharmaceutical company could bottle prayer and market it, we would see prayer accepted overnight. One thing that keeps it out of the scientific eye, however, is a complaint that was originally delivered by Galileo against Kepler. It's the belief in action at a distance. One of the nastiest things you can say about a colleague these days is that he believes in mental action at a distance. Prayer is action at a distance. There is no accepted theory in modern science that says how anything could act at a distance with no energetic signal in between. Prayer is apparently unmediated, and you can't block or shield it. It works as powerfully on the other side of the earth as it does from one inch away.

What about the wave and particle experiments in quantum physics, where the observer changes the effects? The wave becomes the particle, the particle becomes the wave, and there's no visible connection.

Yes, that's true. The area called quantum mechanics in quantum-relativistic physics is alive these days, buzzing about nonlocality.

So this is action at a distance?

This is action at a distance—and it's right at home in the labs of quantum physicists. Whether or not this is going to be the model that carries the day, explaining how prayer might work, is open to question. That probably is the most fertile theory that we could look to in science now. A Nobel physicist, Brian Josephson, has actually proposed that quantum nonlocality lies at the heart of these nonlocal experiences that people have at the psychological, spiritual, and mental levels. There are some pretty heavy-duty people among physicists these days who are looking to quantum physics for explanations about how prayer, clairvoyance, and telepathy might work. I must say that this is speculation at this stage, and whether it proves to be the explanation for prayer, remains to be seen.

You mentioned that prayer might produce a placebo effect. I'm thinking of all the scientific studies that have proven that placebos can work to heal. They apparently contribute to an increase in neurotransmitters in the patient's body, which increases healing. It may mean that prayer generates placebo effects.

I'm sure that prayer does generate placebo effects if someone knows they are being prayed for and feel good about it. They get some strong surge of neurotransmitters that perks up their immune systems, and so on. Where this begins to become even more interesting, however, is when the person is prayed for at a distance, is completely unaware that he or she is being prayed for, and something good happens. Then, how do you explain it? In that situation, the person isn't even having the thought that he or she is being prayed for, so that's where the rub comes. Scientifically, I'm almost amused at the trouble that specialists and physicians have over the explanation problem here. I think that our job is to honor the facts that appear in the experiments. If we have an explanation, that's terrific. If we don't, that's no excuse not to honor the facts. Frequently, the explanation comes later. This was so with penicillin. When penicillin was first discovered, we didn't have a clue about how it worked, but it was obvious that it did. The explanation took a long time. I think we're at the same stage with prayer. We have some clues about how it works, but no accepted explanation. That doesn't justify us in tossing out the observation. Our job is to go straight through the data and not go around it. We've got to engage it. I think that's where we are right now with prayer.

Are there studies showing that prayer works in other parts of the world?

Most other cultures aren't sitting around holding their breath waiting to find out what the latest double-blind scientific laboratory study shows. They just go about their prayer. They are really not as infatuated as we are about looking at the science behind this. I know of no other cultures where such a concerted effort has been made to prove prayer in the laboratory. This really brings up some interesting points that have to do with whether or not the Almighty is involved in how prayer works. Most people in our culture probably believe that the Absolute—God, Goddess, or what not—is connected with the power of prayer. There are other cultures, however, who do not believe in a God or a Goddess, in which prayer seems to work just as well.

The most notable example is Buddhism. Buddhism isn't a theistic religion—Buddhists don't hold to the notion of a personal God—but they pray like crazy. They go through life spinning their prayer wheels, and there's no reason to suppose that Buddhist prayers aren't answered. So it challenges us to ask: What do we do with the God concept, with the Goddess concept? Is this central to what we can call the prayer loop? There are a lot of people in our culture who find the idea that prayer could work without God really offensive. I think this is sort of amusing. Most people don't like to learn that the Buddhist prayers work just fine with no God included.

This idea about God is interesting, because again it's this notion that something outside of ourselves will take care of it. You're raising the point with the Buddhist philosophy that there's a power within. Maybe prayer catalyzes that healing power within each of us?

I completely agree with that. Joseph Campbell said that the idea of inner divinity can be found not just in Eastern teachings such as Buddhism and Hinduism, but in Christianity as well. He used to say, "The Bible says the kingdom of heaven is within. Who's in heaven? God! So God is within!" Yet, when Christian mystics have spoken of "the divine within," they have often been accused of heresy and blasphemy. Meister Eckhart was an example in 13th-century Germany. Campbell often wondered why this was so hard for Christians to accept.

You had a chapter in your book Healing Words *about the other side, the dark side of prayer, that prayer can actually bring harm or hurt. What about that?*

If you consider prayer as a therapy, which many people do, this raises the possibility that prayer may have side effects. There are no perfect therapies; all have side effects. I'm convinced, looking at the laboratory evidence, as well as from people's stories, that there is a dark side, a shadow side to prayer. Studies actually show that if the praying person in the lab experiment switches his or her intentions from a loving, empathic, compassionate state to a negative or hateful state, the subjects are harmed. These invariably involve lower organisms such as mice, bacteria, fungi, and so on. You can't test negative prayer on humans because it's unethical and illegal. But the bottom line is that you can demonstrate negative effects on living organisms that correspond to negative psychological states. I think these events deserve greater notice. Microorganisms and humans share common biochemical processes. If you can harm bacteria, you should suspect you can also harm human beings, whose biochemistry can be identical. People seem to believe this. In 1994, a Gallup poll revealed that 5 percent of the Americans surveyed had prayed for harm to other individuals—and that's just the one-in-twenty who will admit it.

If you look around the world anthropologically, you can find some dramatic examples of this. The most smashing one I came up with doing this research is a custom in the Hawaiian tradition that was actually called the death prayer. In this custom, the *kahuna* shamans would gather together on an island and actually pray for the death of a person on a distant island who was completely unaware that this was going on. In all fairness, we should say that they would never use this negative prayer, this death prayer, unless this victim was raising some real stink in the culture and would not respond to any other form of coercion. They would basically dispose of him at a distance. Strictly speaking, this is not classical voodoo, because in voodoo, the subject is generally informed that he or she has been hexed, and cooperates with the dire prediction, often dying. In the death prayer, it's clear that the victim often did not know he or she had been cursed.

This is the same thing with the Jivaro, right?

Exactly. Actually, Michael Harner, who lived with them for many years in the jungles of the Amazon, affirmed seeing this going on there. It turns out that in Hawaii, the victims of this death prayer frequently die in the same way. This is a striking observation. The way they die is a dead ringer for a disease that currently exists in modern medicine for which we have no explanation. It's called the Guillain-Barré syndrome. The feet go to sleep, the toes become numb, the feet become paralyzed, and the numbness and paralysis rise up from the lower extremities to the trunk. When it reaches the level of the diaphragm, the victim can no longer breathe and dies from suffocation.

Today, we regard this as a disease of unknown origin. We put people on mechanical respirators to keep them alive until this disease goes away. I think that we need to give real consideration to whether or not this particular disease, and maybe other diseases of unknown origin, could be due to these negative psychological influences. I think this possibility has been affirmed in almost every culture that has ever existed—except ours.

I'm reminded once again of how soul *is coming up more and more in our culture, and that certainly has something to do with healing and prayer, doesn't it?*

Actually, this brings up what I think is the major payoff of prayer. If we pray for a cancer to go away or a heart attack to heal, and it does, we can be grateful. But there is a sense in which prayer's benefits transcend the eradication of illness. Prayer's most majestic function is to connect us with the Absolute—to something eternal and immortal, to something wiser and greater than the individual self. The lab experiments in prayer can help us make this leap of understanding. The fact that prayer works at a distance suggests strongly that there is some aspect of our consciousness that extends beyond our body and is thus more than the physical. Something about us appears unrestricted in space and time. This quality of consciousness appears *nonlocal*—unconfinable by space and time. This aspect of the mind has generally been called the soul—something eternal and immortal, something beyond the physical.

In fact, the lab experiments in distant, intercessory prayer are empirical, indirect evidence for a soul-like quality in humans. That is one reason they are so important. We have always regarded belief in the soul as fantasy. Today we can point to actual indirect evidence and say that belief in the soul is not just wishful thinking.

Again: If we pray for a healing and the disease goes away, that's a blessing and a grace. But if the disease escalates and we die, we shall have to settle for immortality. Not a bad consolation prize!

How do you mean?

Manley P. Hall once said, "There is a type of person in whose mind God is always getting mixed up with vitamins." He was trying to warn his students against "using God" in a strictly utilitarian, instrumental way. This problem is ancient. Meister Eckhart, in 13th-century Germany, said, "Most people use God like a cow—for the milk and cheese He can produce." We continually need to examine what we think prayer is "for." Is it a way of getting things? Think of the Big Three things most people are striving for—health and longevity, prosperity, and fulfilling relationships. We can pray to be blessed with such things; it's our nature to do so. But these are minor compared with the larger lesson of prayer—which is to reveal to us that we're *already* divine, eternal, and immortal.

You know, we ought to think about the origin of the word *utopia*. It means "not in a place." If utopia is not in a place, it's not in a particular time. This means that utopia, if it exists, is here and now. We're not talking salvation, but *enlightenment*—waking up to the fact of inner divinity, the indwelling Christ, the God within. As the Hindus say "Tat tvam asi!"—you're it! Prayer can help us reach this understanding. But the best way to sabotage this majestic function of prayer is always to "use God as a cow," or to "confuse God with vitamins."

I remember that there was a time in my life when I was studying what prayer was really about. I remember reading a description of how to pray. There was this idea that you pray, and then you imagine yourself as already having the result of the prayer. That is, you let yourself experience the quality of the feeling that will come as a result of the prayer. Then you let go of it, you detach yourself from it. Very Buddhist, very Christian—a Buddhist idea in the Christian context. Because I was reading a Christian description of what prayer was, and then that took me to one of those unclear-on-the-concept cartoons, I think it was "Ziggy" or something. Ziggy's been praying, he's in the middle of the cathedral, and he's saying, "Why me?" and then the roof opens up, and down through the roof comes a voice saying,

"Because you bug me." This is constantly praying to the external. Prayer is really looking for that place within where we can be. It's somehow been misinterpreted to mean that you pray to something, for something, and that's externalizing it.

That's exactly right. It's interesting to look at some of the research showing the relative effectiveness of different prayer strategies in a series of experiments with germinating seeds. The most effective prayer strategy was that in which the person really asked for nothing. In one phase of the experiment the person prayed for an increased germination rate. In a different phase, he or she simply prayed, "Thy will be done" or "May the best thing happen."When the individual did not make a specific demand through prayer, the results were considerably more effective than when a specific outcome was requested. This is evidence that *nonattachment* is really important; it's more than a nice metaphor. "Letting go" can be better than "holding on" or trying aggressively to "make it happen."

But there really is no formula for how to pray. Other studies indicate that the directed way of praying, imaging, and visualizing, in which one specifies the desired outcome, are more effective than the open-ended approach. Which way should we pray? It depends, I feel, on the personality and temperament of the praying individual. Most extroverts like to use a strategy that specifies the outcome. Introverts, in contrast, feel better "leaving it up to a higher power" and praying "Thy will be done." Above all, we must look in our hearts, not to science, for guidance in how to pray. The bottom line is that both methods work. It's up to us to find the method that best fulfills our needs and honors who we are.

Dr. Ann Ulanov, a well-known theologian, was once asked in a lecture, "How should I pray?" She responded, "It's so simple. Ask God." This captures an important point. Don't try to find out how to pray in books or in lab experiments. Look to your heart and to the Divine. We ought to relax and lighten up on this score. The Universe does not depend on whether or not we get it right in prayer.

We are hopeful about seeing more doctors come forward to say, "Let's use prayer," and so forth. What are we going to see in the medical area?

We're not going to see doctors waking up overnight on this. What we are going to see is medicine changing because of pressures and developments—not so much from the inside, but from the outside. If you look at people who have turned out this data, most of them are not on anybody's faculties at major medical schools. If you look at the pressures that were exerted to form the Office of Alternative Medicine, it was people demanding alternative medicine methods of therapy. It's interesting to note that this office was established not because anybody within the National Institutes of Health [NIH] had sudden radical enlightenment over these issues. This office came about because of people outside the NIH, people who recognized the value of these alternative medicines in their own lives. That's where the potent pressures are coming now—it's from scientists on the margins of science and from real folks. I must say, if I could give a plug for this Office of Alternative Medicine, the first thing I would suggest is to pray. Secondly, people could write their congressional representatives to inform them that this new Office of Alternative Medicine exists. It is so new that congresspeople actually don't know that it's there at the NIH. And while they're at it, the people who write their congressmen and congresswomen could also ask for generous funding for this office.

How do you see prayer and medicine integrating in the future?

There is so much experimental data supporting the effects of prayer that we can predict that its use in medicine is going to increase. The avalanche of data supporting it will continue. If prayer becomes the established norm in a community, will those physicians who do not at least mention it as a possible resource be judged guilty of malpractice? This is a serious question. Currently, 11 medical schools have courses in "spirituality in clinical medicine," and more are developing these programs. My advice is: Hang on to your hats. Prayer is back in medicine. At long last, the taboo on spirituality is broken.

EPILOGUE

Prayer is good for you. Most particularly, we would see headlines everywhere about the new breakthrough in medicine if the scientifically validated results of prayer to heal were a pill. However, this doesn't occur because of the continued conventional wisdom that is locked into scientific materialism. If we can't see it, touch it, smell it, or taste it, then somehow it's not real and we should dismiss it as irrelevant. The immense value of Larry Dossey's message is that here is a medical doctor telling us that prayer works and who is providing the scientific research to back it up.

A recent survey of physicians reported in the *Christian Science Monitor* revealed that 99 percent of them believe patients' religious beliefs can contribute in a positive way to the healing process. Moreover, 92 percent said they have had patients who sought the aid of a spiritual leader to help with their medical condition. Dossey confirms this trend with the work he is doing and writing about. Clearly, we, as patients and potential patients are the beneficiaries.

CHAPTER TWO

FALLING AWAKE
THROUGH MEDITATION

Jon Kabat-Zinn, with Michael Toms

PROLOGUE

*T*here's nothing wrong with thinking; it goes on all the time
inside our minds. The question is whether the thinking
process becomes the sum total of our lives. Are we living in our
heads, or are we truly experiencing life in all its richness? The
answer to these questions, and to discovering what it means to be
fully awake in each moment, lies in mindfulness—perceiving the
extraordinary vividness of the here and now—neither in the past
nor in the future, but present and fully awake. When we can do
this, the quality of our moments and our life actually changes.
Mindfulness can enable us to more effectively face life's challenges and to fully embrace the ups and downs of life's journey.

All types of people in all walks of life can benefit from the practice of mindfulness.

Jon Kabat-Zinn has helped train executives, medical students, prisoners, physicians, hospital employees, Olympic athletes, judges, and Catholic priests. He is the founder and director of the Stress Reduction Clinic at the University of Massachusetts Medical Center; Executive Director of its Center for Mindfulness in Medicine, Health Care, and Society; and an Associate Professor of Medicine in the Division of Preventive and Behavioral Medicine. His clinic was featured in 1993 in the PBS series "Healing and the Mind" with Bill Moyers. He is the author of Full Catastrophe Living: Using the Wisdom of Your Body and Mind to Face Stress, Pain, and Illness; Wherever You Go, There You Are: Mindfulness Meditation in Everyday Life; *and co-author, with his wife, Myla, of* Everyday Blessings: The Inner Work of Mindful Parenting.

MICHAEL TOMS: *Jon, how did you first encounter the idea of mindfulness, the practice?*

JON KABAT-ZINN: I'm not sure I even remember. There was a time when I was a graduate student at MIT, early on in the mid-sixties, when I was very dissatisfied with a lot of things going on in my life. It was right after the Gulf of Tonkin incident, and there was an awful lot of turmoil going on in the country in the Civil Rights movement, and then the growing anti-war movement. I was at MIT, which was deeply involved in making the new generation of smart weapons that were being used in Vietnam. I was looking for some way to make sense of it all. I was studying molecular biology, and it seemed to me that, as scientists, we were only looking at certain aspects of living systems and really ignoring other aspects of life totally, such as who we are and how we come to be conscious.

I went to MIT, in my naive enthusiasm, to study the biology of consciousness, and I found that there was really no way to do it there. But it was wonderful to be in Cambridge at that time since every swami, Zen master, guru, and rinpoche in the world was coming through—giving talks and workshops, parading their wares, you might say. It was fascinating. I felt that while I was doing science with one part of my being, I also had a strong yearning to find out what the rest of the world knew that maybe scientists didn't about other aspects of consciousness. So I started pursuing this kind of stuff on the side. When I started practicing martial arts—Okinawan karate at the time—it turned out that they were doing hatha yoga for warm-ups, and that's how I was exposed to it for the first time. Over time, there were a lot of different elements to it that eventually led to my own daily meditation practice, first in the Zen tradition, later in the Vipassana tradition. I came to see and feel that the core of all of the Buddhist teachings, and of the yoga teachings, was awareness—with the moment-to-moment nonjudgmental awareness known as *mindfulness.*

In your books Full Catastrophe Living *and* Wherever You Go There You Are, *you point out that you don't really have to become a Buddhist to practice mindfulness.*

Exactly. I think that there are universal aspects to meditation that, as a culture, we are starving for. You might say we've become denatured on certain wavelengths in terms of our relationship to the world, and particularly in regard to our own inner experience. We tune out a great deal, we take a great deal for granted, and, as Americans, as a culture, we're very hard driving. We're always moving someplace else, progressing, trying to make things better.

I set up the Stress Reduction Clinic at the University of Massachusetts Medical Center back in 1979, basically as an experiment, a sort of a tentative demonstration project to take what I understood to be the essence of meditative practice within the Buddhist and yogic traditions and offer it within the mainstream. The hope was that regular folks would find it relevant to their lives and be motivated to actually practice it in the same way that people are motivated within the more traditional and monastic traditions. That turned out to be the case. What we found was that people of all different ages from all walks of life, who were not the slightest bit interested in enlightenment or in Zen or in meditation or anything like that, actually found it to be tremendously valuable and relevant in their lives—when it was encountered in a context that included a physician referral to a "stress reduction" clinic within the hospital. That clinic took the form of an eight-week course designed to teach people how to take better care of themselves as a complement to whatever health care and medicine was doing for them—a participatory model of health care.

One way I describe the vision, out of which the clinic came, is that if you think about it for a moment, hospitals really function as "dukkha magnets." *Dukkha* is the Buddhist term for suffering. It means not just anguish, but also an out-of-jointness due to impermanence, to the inevitability of change. When dukkha reaches a very high level, people either get taken to the morgue or to the hospital. And since it's really hard to work with people once they've been taken to the morgue, the hospital seemed like a perfect place to introduce a learning experience about dealing consciously with suffering and with pain and stress (which you might call the closest Western term to dukkha) in such a way that people would, in fact, come out of the hospital with greater levels of understanding and wisdom about how to regulate their responses to things that they were unable to change—things that were under their control that might be compounding their pain and their suffering.

You did some studies about applying the practice of mindfulness to chronic pain?

Yes. We started out studying the effects of meditation training on people with chronic pain, and then branched out to a number of other research areas as well. It seemed from the beginning that it would be irresponsible to do this kind of work clinically without making the effort to document the results, and then write them up in a scientifically rigorous way so that we could get the word out. In a way, we hoped it would be a way of influencing the thinking in science and medicine about what might be possible around the whole issue of people accessing their own deep inner resources for healing through their capacity for greater intentionality and consciousness, or whatever you want to call it—the power of the mind/body connection for growing, for learning, for healing, for lifestyle change, for all the good things that doctors are sometimes desperate to have their patients do, but which are actually very hard to get anybody to make changes in—particularly in the area of profound attitudinal and behavioral changes.

Can you give us an example of the results with someone who was suffering from chronic pain?

We found right away, even before we started doing formal studies, that people would come in with relatively high levels of symptoms of all kinds—not just physical discomfort and physical symptoms, but also with high levels of psychological distress, which frequently took the form of anxiety, panic, irritability, and somatization. They were not responding fully to their medical treatments. They were being maintained at a particular level of distress and pain, often very inadequate, and lacked a sense of being satisfied in the way they were being treated by the health-care system.

So our clinic was basically set up as a net to catch people

falling through the cracks of the health-care system—people who were dissatisfied with the outcome of their treatment and, once we had caught them, to challenge them to do something differently, to do something for themselves that no one on the planet could do for them, as a *complement* to the care they were receiving, if any, from the health-care system.

What we saw over a period of eight weeks was a rapid decrease in both the physical and psychological symptoms that people were having, including present-moment pain, and the way they saw and thought about the parts of their body that were causing them the most problems. That kind of change was not observed in chronic-pain patients who were going through a traditional pain clinic and undergoing high-tech medical interventions. So there seemed to be something important about participating in a learning-based intervention grounded in mindfulness training—this is really an educational or self-educational model rather than a traditional group therapy or even therapeutic model. People train in awareness of the mind/body interface and can discover for themselves that, even with a lot of pain, it is actually possible to reduce pain itself and the suffering associated with pain. In long-term follow-up studies, we later showed that those reductions in pain and distress were maintained up to four years later, and that people attributed a great deal of the improvement in their pain levels to their participation in this program. And many continue to report improvements even now, up to 18 years later.

That doesn't mean, by the way, that the pain magically disappears, or that you can just "meditate away" all your pain, or that if you've had three back surgeries or you've injured your back or your neck, meditation is the answer to all life's problems and it's just going to make everything clear up and go away and you'll be back in your old body. It doesn't mean that at all. What it basically means is that if pain is a part of your experience in life and in your body, you can learn to work with it in certain ways. We're teaching people the "how" of working with it; there's no promise that their pain will magically clear up. But we see two things: One is that in many cases pain levels are lowered. But another even more profound thing is that people change their relationship to their pain, even when it doesn't improve. As a consequence, they can feel much more in control of it.

The idea of coming together as a group to deal with the issue of pain in a hospital setting is interesting. It also reminds me of David Spiegel's work with women who have breast cancer. Just having a support group where these women are able to talk about what they're dealing with enables them to survive longer.

That's an important point—just having a caring environment in which you can express your feelings and be heard and accepted for who you are is profoundly healing. People who have pain don't talk about it most of the time because they've usually learned a long time ago that no one wants to hear about it. Coming to the hospital and being able to actually talk about your experience—and in a framework in which you know you're not going to be judged—is very powerful and affirming. People know they're not going to be condemned for being real.

Some kinds of psychological interventions for pain are based on an operant conditioning model that says that pain is a learned behavior, and you can unlearn it in an environment where the word *pain* is no longer used and nothing contributes to identification with that experience as "pain." It's a lot like treating somebody like a rat in a cage, and many of our patients report that it's very demeaning. It can be effective with some people, but I prefer a model that allows for the full expression of present-moment experience. Then, we work with whatever comes up so that we don't get attached to pain or absence of pain.

I might also point out that our studies in the field of pain were only the beginning of the research that we have been doing over the years in the clinic. One unusual aspect of our program is that we don't just conduct mindfulness-based stress reduction programs for people with chronic pain. People are referred to the clinic with AIDS, heart disease, cancer, hypertension, skin disorders, headaches, and every conceivable diagnosis and malady. They all go through the same program together, regardless of their diagnoses. In this way, at least, it's very different from the program described in the Spiegel study, which was conducted only on women with stage-four breast cancer. Moreover, that approach is a kind of small-group therapy known as supportive emotive therapy. Our program is based on intensive training in mindfulness meditation in a large group setting. The classes do develop a unique kind of community in which deep emotion can be expressed and supported, but talking about our feelings and supporting each other is not the primary focus. The focus is on how we might work with our feelings within the context of mindfulness meditation practice itself. We are now well along in a study of women with early-stage breast cancer—looking at the effects of our eight-week intervention, which is much shorter than the original Spiegel intervention.

A lot of people have the idea that somehow the practice of meditation requires shutting the world out and stopping our thinking. What about those misconceptions?

I have a little *Bazooka Joe* comic from a bubblegum wrapper that one of my patients brought me once, which I often use in professional lectures such as Medical Grand Rounds. One of the characters is shown sitting. His friends come up and say: "What are you up to, Mort?" to which he replies, "Practicing meditation. It fills me with inner peace. After two minutes, my mind is a compete blank." In the last picture, the friends are shown walking away, with one saying, "Gee, and I thought he was born that way!"

It's a very deep misconception that meditation is about making your mind blank, that it involves shutting off or pushing away

things so that you can achieve some kind of deeper, more desirable state of clarity and calmness. It's not that those deeper, more
desirable states of clarity and calmness do not exist and cannot be
cultivated—they can. But it is a kind of learning that in some
ways is akin to falling asleep—although meditation is really
about "falling awake." If you try too hard to get to sleep, chances
are you are not going to fall asleep at all. People have that experience all the time, of having a lot to do the next day—big meetings, high stakes. You get into bed just like you do every other
night and shut off the lights, but what doesn't shut off are the
inner lights. The mind won't shut down. The more you try to
force yourself to go to sleep, the less you will be able to.

I like to describe the mind as being like the surface of the
ocean—it's just in the nature of water to wave. And it is part of
the nature of our minds to wave as well. The mind waves virtually all the time. If you try to shut off the waves, it's a bit like trying to put a glass plate over the ocean to stop it from being as it
is. It's not going to work very well.

Let's take the ocean analogy a little bit further. If you identify
with the entire body of water, rather than just with the waves at the
surface, then you will know that the movement is at most 10 or 20
feet down or so. The movement is at most a gentle undulation, and
there is a great calmness even when the surface is whipped up by
violent storms. Well, the mind is the same way. It goes through all
sorts of storms of one kind or another. The surface can be highly
agitated and reactive, yet there is all the while another element of
mind that is always present but that we just don't visit very often,
and that we may not be entirely familiar with, which stays calm,
stable, and balanced even in the midst of all that.

So the matter of inner peace is not getting it, so to speak, but
uncovering it, because it's there all the time. Meditation is really
the practice of allowing yourself to just *be,* and being comfortable with *whatever* comes up. That does require some practice.
It's a discipline. Just as in lifting weights, if you hope to have big-

ger biceps, you've got to work with the resistance of the weights themselves in order to have biceps grow.

Qualities of concentration, equanimity, calmness, and insight do grow as you work against the resistance that you find in the present moment—both in the outer world and in the mind. That's what the real work is about. Really, it is an adventure. It can be a hell of a lot of fun—and it can be hell. You have to be willing to face what I call the "full catastrophe"—the full extent of the human condition—moment by moment in your life, whatever comes up. Our patients come to us expecting to get relaxed. In fact, one of the names of our program is the Stress Reduction and Relaxation Program; so, in a sense, we are setting people up to expect "relaxation" and to expect "stress reduction."

But the real message is that the way to stress reduction, or relaxation, is to not try to get anywhere. And this is a little bit of a stretch for people at first because it's a principle we're not exactly taught in elementary school. But people very quickly pick up that it's similar to what we just said about falling asleep—only this is actually falling awake. Thich Nhat Hanh uses a beautiful image: watering the seeds of mindfulness. The reason we need to water those seeds in ourselves constantly, if we hope for them to germinate and sprout, if we hope to *cultivate* them, is in part because that is the very nature of all growth and learning—it has to be nourished and protected. On the other hand, it's also true that most of the time we're watering the weeds; we're watering seeds of suffering and mindlessness by being reactive, by living on automatic pilot, by letting our present moments be squeezed out by our ambitions, our fears, our memories, and so forth.

There's the critique of such practices, particularly with many of them rooted in Oriental and Asian religions, that somehow because of the lifestyle we have here in the West, and the way we pace our lives, and the kind of business activity we're involved in, that it's really not possible for us to practice what is being called mindfulness because their lifestyle is different. What are your thoughts on this?

I think we're on very safe ground in saying that we've proven that it is possible. People of all walks of life and all ages start practicing with us in our clinic, or they come to the practice through books and tapes. Ten years later, or more, many people tell us they're still practicing, and many say that they have missed very few days. Many of these people are in prominent positions in companies. Or they are scientists, doctors, lawyers, teachers, firefighters, cops, construction workers—and I think this culture is not only fertile ground for mindfulness, but a culture actually starving for mindfulness.

We see this hunger, this yearning for authentic experience and for inner peace, in the prisons; we see it in our work in the inner city, we see it in the clinic, and we see it in schools with young children. So, it seems to me that the sense that you have to have a certain kind of cultural preparation for this kind of thing to happen belies the fact that this practice, whatever you want to call it, has spread throughout many different cultures and many different countries in the Orient over the past 2,500 years. Every time, it went through a transformation in which it took on some elements of the host culture. But the essence was never lost. Of course, it also went through the same kind of political machinations that any other cultural emergence would go through, but there's always been at least some elements of clarity and purity that have come through. I think this is because paying attention, which is what meditation is really about, is absolutely fundamental to our nature as human beings.

Taking five minutes in the early morning just before you begin your day can be useful.

Absolutely. You might think of it as "tuning the instrument." If you really want to play something on the violin, it's helpful to tune the instrument first. In many ways, the body can be seen as an instrument. I like to know how mine is in the morning. When you start to meditate and do yoga and bring a certain awareness to your body, you'll notice that not only is it different every day when you wake up, but it's different virtually from moment to moment. And if you can know something about this, you can use that knowledge to your advantage. This is particularly true for people who have health problems and who have good days and bad days. Very often the mind can trigger a bad day even before it has started. We often wake up anxious before our feet hit the floor. We're already running, often running on empty, and as you say, five minutes or even five seconds before you get out of bed, bringing your attention to the breath, and to a sense of your body lying here, just experiencing the sensations in your body, the whole of your body breathing, can be very useful.

Coming back to your breath, affirming that you're awake even before you get out of bed, can lead to grounding your day in mindfulness. Then, when you take a shower, you can check and see if you're really in the shower—a lot of people, including myself sometimes, are already at work. The body's in the shower, but the mind is someplace else. Once you've become more familiar with the possibility of being present for all your moments, you can bring yourself back when you go off. It's not bad that the mind is at work. It's perfectly understandable; but if your mind is always someplace else, then the consequences of that are going to be very unfortunate. You may miss almost everything that's of any meaning. So it's a very beautiful practice to take every moment, if you will, as if it's your last moment, and live it as fully as possible. Then, I think, death would take care of itself, and life would really be an adventure.

So there's a real teaching here, particularly for anyone who's consulting with a physician, to make sure that the doctor or other health professional is really listening.

Absolutely. I don't think it hurts to be more assertive. You know, it's very intimidating when somebody has a white coat on and they have all the power, and they seemingly have all the knowledge. But you have to remember as a patient, as a client, that they are basically working for you. I think it's very important, if you don't understand something and you want to understand it, to ask about it. Or, if you feel that someone's not paying attention, trust yourself enough and have enough confidence in yourself to just check and say, "Are you really hearing what I'm saying?" You don't have to do it in a hostile way. It calls for being assertive rather than aggressive. It can be very threatening to physicians when you do that, and sometimes people need to change their doctors if they are not receptive to that kind of respectful partnership.

If you don't feel comfortable with your doctor, you might at least explore the question of whether you should be seeing someone else. Sometimes a doctor is so good technically that you might decide, "Well, I don't need my surgeon to be that sensitive; I'll be sensitive myself and just let the surgeon do the cutting and the sewing in a good way." Now, that's fine, but I think there are many cases—I see them all the time—of people who are in miserable relationships with their health-care providers. They really do better when they find somebody who will listen more.

When you first came to the University of Massachusetts Medical Center, you were given a white coat. What did you do?

I hung it on the back of my door, and I've never used it in 18 years. I've got three of them, actually, with nice embroidery that says "Dr. Kabat-Zinn, Department of Medicine." The white coat functions for doctors as a positive placebo because it's a symbol of authority and knowledge, and it is very reassuring. But my job in the Stress-Reduction Clinic is to teach people to be the authority on their own life and their own body. I really believe—and I think most doctors do—that fundamentally, patients know an enormous amount about their own bodies. They take it home at night. The doctor doesn't go home at night with them. So one of the challenges in the Stress-Reduction Clinic is to become, if you will, a scientist of your own mind and body. That means suspending judgment and giving a certain kind of dispassionate observation, from moment to moment, of the unfolding of your own experience. When you do that, you can really learn from your own body. With the mindfulness instructions and the kind of meditation instructions that we give to people, over a relatively short period of time, you come to see that you have a very profound role to play in your own growth and healing.

One of the things you touched on in Wherever You Go There You Are *was the aspect of nondoing. In this culture, of course, we have the Judeo-Christian work ethic—that it's important for us to be busy. And some of us feel guilty when we're not busy. What is nondoing? It sounds like it goes against the grain of our acculturation.*

It does, and that's why there are four chapters on it in the book. It's really a plea, if you will, that we take some time every day to stop doing all the doing that we do, which is usually driven by an inner mind state. I mean, you can say what you will about the cultural work ethic and everything else, but we've bought into it so much that it's become internalized. We don't even feel comfortable when we stop. Some people find being on vacation to be unbelievably stressful because they don't know what to do with themselves. It's as if we become our work, and we are very addicted to it, to busyness, to always moving ahead.

Workaholism is a major disease in our society. We get a lot done, but often we don't know who's doing the doing. We are not called human *doings,* by the way, although maybe we should be. We are human *beings*, yet often we don't leave any time for being, especially any wakeful time. We fall into bed exhausted, and as we said, we're up and our feet hit the floor before we know we're even awake or alive. It's one day after another after another. And zap, 20 years can go by easily like that. You may get a lot done on one level, but you may not be in touch at all with what it all means, or what you have even done (and not done—the road not taken). If, on the other hand, you carve out some time every day for what we call "nondoing," you find that it has a certain architecture to it, and is very, very rich. It's not the same as doing nothing. It has its own inner landscape, so to speak. It's not just Oriental or Asian.

Thoreau was deeply involved in nondoing. Anybody who cares to can go back and read *Walden* and see the beauty and the joy and the scientific precision that came out of Thoreau's love of the present moment, his careful observing of the leaves turning color, or watching the fog for an entire day, or listening to the ice thaw. He had nothing to do, so he could do whatever the moment presented, in a wakeful appreciation of that kind of thing. In many ways, this contemplative mind feeds doing in ways that are coherent and bring meaning to the doing. So practicing nondoing is not the same as advocating that we all become vegetables or anything like that. What I'm advocating is that we let our actions come out of nondoing.

At the highest level of sports performance, or dance, or any kind of performing art, if you talk to the artists or performers, they will often say that they can't claim full credit for doing it, that it "just happened." Of course, it "happened" because of all of their training—years and years of training. But it is possible to reach a point where at times it just flows out of your being, out of your fingertips. Anybody who has had a taste of mastery in any domain knows that it's an experience that transcends thinking, even beyond intending. If you actually practice mindfulness, you can shift the probability that such moments will occur and will be available for you to use. We actually train Olympic athletes and other performers in this kind of thing. We're also working with the Chicago Bulls basketball team. We are able to shift the probability of those kinds of clicks happenings—often called being in "the zone," within the sports domain—where mind and body and space and the ball and the opposition, or whatever, come together, and you're in tune with an intuitive knowing. That doesn't come out of trying to make anything happen, but actually seeing what's already happening with a certain precision. Of course, the talent has to be there as well, and then this kind of doing can call it forth more reliably, perhaps.

Your mentioning Thoreau reminds me that he was very connected with Ralph Waldo Emerson and the transcendental movement. I think of John Muir here on the West Coast, kind of a Western Thoreau, although he's from Wisconsin originally. This is a kind of paradox: Thoreau was practicing mindfulness, yet mindfulness is not about transcending life.

Exactly. I think Thoreau knew that, and Emerson as well. There's an appreciation for everything being embedded in everything else so that although they were labeled transcendentalists, what they were really talking about was this appreciation of levels of wholeness, where everything is embedded into everything else. Part of the fun is actually seeing it all simultaneously on a lot of different levels and being able to hold that in awareness and appreciation. Thoreau quotes passages from Chinese sages and from the Upanishads. He was quite familiar with Eastern wisdom traditions. Also, the Native American tradition really was in touch with the notion that there are a lot of different worlds, and we can't dominate nature. In fact, we denature our own being when we restrict ourselves to seeing in one particular way. What mindfulness can do is take the veil off of our seeing, so that a range of different dimensions is accessible to us. Then, we work with them in ways that make for appropriate action in the world.

Buckminster Fuller was someone who really exemplified being in this life as fully as he could be. Again, there's the paradox about being totally engaged in our work, but in a way that when who we are and our work are really connected, then our life is one, and we don't really view what we're doing as work.

Life becomes play, or becomes practice; in some way it becomes meditation. At work we speak of it as "the Tao of work." It is possible to be so into what one's doing and so in love with the beauty of that, that it goes beyond any ego involvement. There is just the beauty of it. This can be experienced alone, or in a whole group of people working together. In Buckminster Fuller's case, the beauty of the laws of form was intoxicating. It was a wonder to him, and what he was basically doing was trying to elaborate and identify and apply those laws as he was discovering them in nature. That's the highest scientific experience of insight and joy—the joy of insight into nature—and this can happen virtually in any place or job if we begin to think of work somewhat differently. The most stressful jobs are those that have little decision-making latitude. In other words, you can't control the work at all, but you have very high demands on you to perform. That can be extremely stressful.

If you have high demands on you, but you also have a degree of control over your hours, and what you'll do or not do, and when you will do this or that, then you can deal with very high levels of demand and not experience so much distress. The addictive aspects of work that I was talking about are when you become so absorbed and intoxicated that you're not attending to other aspects of your life that may be equally important. For example, some people are totally self-destructive in terms of their bodies. They'll be geniuses in one realm and complete idiots in others, with their heads buried in the sand. We can all be totally blind to certain aspects of our own lives. We can easily be out of touch, for instance, with our children or our spouses, and cause them a lot of hurt because we get carried away by our own momentum, and it is intoxicating. Just like alcohol or drugs, it can be misused. Obviously, we all need to decide for ourselves where we are going to put our energy and what's important to us, but I think that if we approach the whole question of work mindfully, we can bring a certain kind of attention to the question of what am I supposed to be doing on the planet, and what is my job, with a capital *J*.

I think more and more as we move into the information age and less and less into the kind of work that was done in the early part of the Industrial Revolution, that more and more people are going to have latitude and control over the question of what is possible in their lives. If you don't want to end up doing somebody else's job on the planet, rather than your own, you can work to shape a reality that is more consistent with your life needs and your soul needs, if you have your finger in the wind, so to speak, if you're asking yourself, "Is this the job that I'm supposed to be doing?" Because there's nothing more painful than doing somebody else's job.

That's where Buckminster Fuller's insight comes in. At one point, he was going to commit suicide because everything that he had touched had turned to dust. As you know, later on he got accolades for all of the creative things that he did; he was far ahead of his time. Now we know that even viruses are constructed using the geometry of dodecahedron, the very geodesic structures that so fascinated Fuller. Now, there is a whole new field of organic chemistry studying carbon compounds in the form of soccer balls and other kinds of elaborate structures, known as buckminster-fullerenes, Bucky Balls, Bucky Tubes, and other things like that. The point is that he had a certain trust and faith in his own genius. He decided not to commit suicide but instead to pretend that he had, and say, "Well, since I'm dead, it doesn't matter if I succeed or fail. From now on, I will devote myself to asking the question, 'What is there on the planet that needs doing, that no one else is doing, and that I care about and have something to say about?' Let me just put my energy into that. Whether it fails or succeeds is now immaterial because, you know, I'm already dead."

That's very similar to the Zen approach, which says: "He who dies before he dies doesn't die when he dies." It has to do with that aspect of the mind that clings to the pronouns *I, me,* and *mine,* inflates them, reifies them, and in the process, makes us lose ourselves and delude ourselves to the point where we will kill each other for trivial slights to our insecure sense of self.

It's also interesting to note that when Bucky made that decision to live his life in a different way and to serve humanity, he didn't just go off and start doing, *but rather, he took over a year of silence where he didn't speak; that was a real practice in mindfulness.*

Yes. And Descartes did that as well. He went off for a long period of time, having realized that he didn't know anything, in an attempt to examine what it was that he actually knew without any more input. There's no sense in comparing ourselves with René Descartes or Buckminster Fuller, but Fuller was adamant that he was nothing special, and that if he could be creative, any-body could be.

He always talked about what "the little individual" can do.

Exactly. My view, which stems in part from working with thousands of people in our clinic, is that human beings truly are geniuses. We are all geniuses, walking miracles, yet we're com-pletely out of touch with the beautiful ways in which our ner-vous system works, and our liver works, and our hearing works, and our eyesight works. We take all that for granted, and we don't realize that there's genius even in our molecular biology and neurobiology.

Life gives rise to emergent phenomena. New things appear out of the complex structure of mind and brain, giving rise to incredible possibilities that are only available if we start to pay attention to the field of unlimited possibilities. Otherwise, we become our own worst enemies and continually get in our own way, and then wind up blaming the rest of the world when we do not succeed in one way or another. I think that people who have made a certain kind of break with the ordinary way of doing work can be real role models. I'm not suggesting that anyone do it the way Buckminster Fuller did, but maybe each of us needs to do it our own way—and we need to find out what that way is, through inquiry and awareness.

There was a great little piece in your book Wherever You Go, There You Are, *called "cat food lessons." Tell us about cat food lessons.*

That's a personal story. People naively think that meditators don't get angry anymore, or don't have the usual kinds of feelings that other people have. That's completely absurd, of course. I tried to put enough of myself into the book so that people wouldn't project on to me that, "Oh, he's some kind of deep person; he lives a life of total equanimity and never reacts," or anything like that. Very often people in the role of meditation teacher get such things projected onto them.

So, "Cat Food Lessons" and several of the other chapters are my ways to sketch out for other people what can go through my mind at times. In that example, I kept finding dirty cat food dishes in the sink with *our* dishes, which brought up in me feelings of revulsion and anger. Some things really get me, and that was one of them. Actually, by writing about it and looking at it more deeply, it is no longer an issue for me, but I used it then as a way of painting a little snapshot of revulsion/anger/annoyance, and how that can play out in family life. Of course, you can take it personally and get hostile, or start going on about, "Don't I count in the family?" and all of that. Meanwhile, it's just a little cat food dish in the sink. You can take anything and blow it out of proportion, and then have big family fights over it. That chapter outlines my inner process of relating to the cat food dish in the sink. The new book, *Everyday Blessings,* shows many different ways in which mindfulness can enhance our ability to parent wisely and compassionately, and to grow beyond our own small and reactive mind.

EPILOGUE

Even a few minutes a day can help us to lessen our anxiety levels, attain inner peace, and enrich the quality of our everyday lives. Through meditation and mindfulness, it is possible to make every moment count, even the ones we spend on such seemingly mundane activities as eating, washing dishes, or driving a car. Jon Kabat-Zinn gives a grounded and practical approach to healing our hectic lives, to reducing the rapid pace, and discovering how through concentration and greater awareness we can dramatically alter our perception of life around us. And we can see ourselves in new ways. Drawing upon Eastern techniques and wisdom, he also uses the authentically American transcendental traditions of Emerson and Thoreau to show us that this approach has merit and is worthy of exploration. Nothing special is required here. All that is needed is your personal energy and willingness to commit yourself to living more consciously in an age of extravagant distractions.

CHAPTER THREE

THE TRUE NATURE
OF MIND

Sogyal Rinpoche, with Michael Toms

PROLOGUE

*W*hat is the true nature of mind? We move through life acting
and reacting with lifelong mind/brain patterns, and often
we're not aware of the source of our behavior. Observing the
process of how we think, slowing down long enough to notice
what it is we're actually doing in the moment, changing our environment to something or someplace unfamiliar—all are ways to
tame the mind so that we can come more into balance and harmony. The Buddhists have been studying the mind for 2,500
years, and the Tibetan Vajrayana tradition of Buddhism possesses an enormous body of knowledge about the way the human
mind works.

In this chapter, I will be interviewing the Buddhist meditation master, Sogyal Rinpoche. Rinpoche was born in Tibet and raised as a son by one of the most revered spiritual teachers of this century, Jamyang Khyentse Chökyi Lodrö. He continued his spiritual education with Dudjom Rinpoche, Dilgo Khyentse Rinpoche, and many other great masters; studied at university in Delhi and Cambridge; and began to teach in the West in 1974. Rinpoche is the founder and spiritual director, along with H. E. Dzogchen Rinpoche, of Rigpa, an international network of centers and groups that follows the teachings of Buddha under his guidance. Rinpoche teaches widely in Europe, America, Australia, and Asia, leading retreats, participating in conferences, and offering various kinds of training based on his book, The Tibetan Book of Living and Dying.

MICHAEL TOMS: *Rinpoche, many people in these times are concerned with what they should do with their lives. I think of the Buddhist Eight-Fold Path, and one of the principles is Right Living. I'd like to hear what you have to say about Right Living and Right Livelihood and what they really mean.*

SOGYAL RINPOCHE: Our lives these days are so busy, so full of stress, that what we need—more than anything else—is something that can help us cut through the cycle of confusion we find ourselves in, something that can really transform the environment of our minds. It's spiritual practice, and especially meditation, that can help us find the way to begin. How? First of all, by just allowing the mind to settle, with a simple method like "Calm Abiding."[1] Quietly watching the breath, mindful and present, the mind will slowly settle, and we become more whole, more focused, more one-pointed, at rest and at peace. Then it's like

---

[1] Shamatha, or "Tranquillity Meditation."

the picture in a camera that gets sharper and clearer the more you bring it into focus: as our minds are more focused, the confusion and fuzziness of ego begin to dissolve, and so we discover the clarity and insight of "Clear Seeing."[2] Our negativity is disarmed, and with it our frustration, anxiety, hope, fear, insecurity, inhibitions and self-consciousness all dissolve as well.

You see, what counts, in the final analysis, is **how we are**. And when we feel connected to our fundamental goodness, we find that we can actually transform the situations and circumstances of life. Otherwise, we are always subject to their influence, and easily become victims of circumstance. If we have the peace and clarity of meditation practice, then however stressful our world might be, even in the thick of city life, we can transform our minds, and what we find is that when our perception changes, the world around us changes, too.

I remember years ago, when I was a student and lived in London, I used to practice in the mornings, and then go and catch the bus. The bus drivers in London can be quite cranky, rude, and even abusive at times. What I found, and what we can all experience, is that practicing in the mornings can change our whole attitude. We don't take things so personally: we're not so oversensitive, because in the space of meditation, the mind no longer grasps so much, and so there is no longer such a strong ego, that 'poor me' to get hurt. Instead, when the bus driver screamed at me, instinctively I couldn't help thinking about how difficult a time *he* must have been having...who knows what problems he was having at home? Instead of reacting with anger, there was a natural feeling of love and compassion. I could understand the suffering behind his anger, and I could take his anger and embrace it and accept it. And sometimes, by so doing, just that was enough to transform it.

When you really train in spiritual practice, first you receive the teachings, then you go into a special environment of retreat,

---

[2] Vipashyana, or "Insight Meditation."

and practice in proper sessions; then you integrate your practice into ordinary life, keeping the discipline of practice. So you apply the teachings regularly and it becomes a habit. As Shantideva said: "There's nothing that does not grow easier if you get used to it."

As we get used to changing our inner world, then our whole perception will change, and everything becomes transformable.

This is what we need in our world today. In the East—for instance, in a country like Tibet, the whole environment is conducive to a more peaceful way of being, and the way people conduct themselves and live is often according to the Dharma. I think that when the whole culture has that spiritual refinement and civilization, then people don't have to resort to meditation to transform their environment in such an urgent way. The thrust of spirituality is then toward education and compassion, and developing the mind. Meditation and understanding the deeper nature of mind is something that not everybody will feel the need to follow, only those who really dedicate their lives to spiritual practice. Whereas in the West, it's almost a question of survival.

"Right Living" blossoms naturally when meditation has entered our being, and when, with mindfulness, we can transform even the most menial of circumstances into something inspiring. Actually, the Buddhist path is not said to be meditation alone, but three trainings: in discipline, meditation, and wisdom. **Meditation** is the beginning: It's meditation that cuts the cycle, the pattern, of habit, and then gradually transforms the mind, and so inspires **wisdom**. Then, with that greater wisdom and discernment, we can simplify our life more and more, and this becomes the **discipline** of Right Living.

Without the support of discipline, meditation alone will not change our life; it'll change its momentum, but it will not transform it. With the support of **discipline**, our **meditation** deepens, opening our minds to greater **wisdom** and richer insights into how to simplify our lives through **discipline**. And so it deepens, progressively, further and further.

Of course, often it's difficult living up to the teachings, but we should never feel guilty. On the path of meditation, we are not imposing any kind of ideal on ourselves, spiritual or otherwise, but simply sitting quietly and pacifying and purifying our mind to its inherent nature. If we try to apply some kind of ideal, or dogma, it will only deflect and disillusion us. But when we enter into meditation and cultivate compassion, we will realize deeply **why** we have to be ethical. Discipline and a respect for cause and effect will follow quite naturally, because we have seen the wisdom of them.

So it doesn't require attaching oneself to a dogma or a particular doctrine as much as it just involves slowing down a little bit?

It requires slowing down, I think, to start with, because to slow down is to simplify; it's part of discipline. Then, when we slow down, we can allow ourselves to find more inspiration, and so we can hear the teachings much better. This is so important: I can't emphasize it too much. When we're uninspired, we cannot truly hear the teachings, or they somehow fail to touch us deeply. The power of inspiration is tremendous. However confused and agitated our minds may be, at the same time, with the right inspiration, or in the right environment, it is possible to transform them in a matter of minutes, or even seconds.

I remember a student of mine in Paris, a young man, very passionate and headstrong. One evening, he was in a foul mood, agitated and nervous, added to which, he had a splitting headache. Everything had gone wrong that day, and finally he drove me to the hall where we always hold the teachings. He went in and sat down in a seat in the front row. And then it happened. Suddenly, something lifted; I could see it in his face. Even before I had begun to teach. Just to be in that environment had actually transformed the mood in his mind.

So inspiration is the key. I always advise my students to listen to a tape of the teachings when they're going to work or are caught in a traffic jam. They so often find this will bring the inspiration they need to transform their whole frame of mind.

We have more experience of actually living in our lives. When you talk about finding our real nature, the question comes up: What is our real nature? How do we know what our real nature is if we quiet ourselves, if we slow down?

There are many aspects to the mind, but there are two that stand out. The first is the ordinary mind, which we call in Tibetan, "sem." Sem is the mind that thinks, that plots and desires and manipulates, that flares up in anger, that creates and indulges in waves of negative emotions and thoughts, that has to go on and on confirming its "existence" by fragmenting, conceptualizing, and solidifying our experience. Then there is the very nature of mind, its innermost essence; in Tibetan we call it "Rigpa"—a primordial, pure, pristine awareness that is intelligent, cognizant, radiant, and always awake. Under certain special circumstances, some inspiration can uncover glimpses of this nature of mind.

There's an example I often use to depict what happens in meditation practice. In the peace and clarity of meditation, the clouds of our thoughts and emotions begin to dissolve, to reveal the innermost nature of our mind, like a clear and cloudless sky. And there, our true nature, our Buddha nature, shines out, just like the sun. That sun possesses both warmth and light: the warmth of "love-compassion" and the light of wisdom.

In that state, we feel, very simply, so "good." Love and compassion are there, boundless and immeasurable. Generosity just blossoms quite naturally. And there's a certainty, too. When you are in that state, you know, you recognize, without a shadow of doubt, that "this is it."

All the barriers—all those limitations that kept us back from ourselves and others—dissolve. Anger and the negative emotions dissolve, like a fist slowly unclenching, as grasping itself dissolves.

You become more "you," more in touch with yourself, and therefore with everybody else. You discover a new confidence and self-esteem. Because you have conquered yourself, you have conquered the world. Because when you have destroyed the ego, you have destroyed your greatest enemy.

There are moments in this state in which there is not even a memory of pain or suffering. On a deeper level, there is no pain and no suffering, intrinsically; it's all illusory and dreamlike. Whenever we are in touch with the nature of mind, whenever we connect with our fundamental goodness, we are at our best, restored to our true self, and out of this comes tremendous benefit, for both ourselves and others.

Once we have come to recognize and face ourselves, it seems so stupid not to do everything in our power to remain always in this state. Because to live in the light of the nature of mind is to live as a true human being. In moments such as these, we feel at our most inspired ever, but we need constantly to **remember** it, by practicing again and again. Because the trouble is: We forget so often, and so easily.

Rinpoche, you travel throughout the world. You just came back from a trip to Australia, You're on your way to Europe in just a few days. You have centers in four continents that I'm aware of, and you speak and work with people all over the world. Do you notice a difference in the kinds of question or the kinds of concerns that you receive from people who are trying to deepen their spiritual life in Europe versus America versus Australia?

Fundamentally speaking, human beings are the same everywhere, with the same concerns, the same wish to be happy, and the same wish not to suffer. We can speak of "East" and "West," but our basic needs and questions are almost universal. At the same time, of course, there are slight differences in people's ways of thinking and perceiving, and in the way they'll ask questions. The Australians will have their own particular style and way of putting questions; the Americans will have another, and so will the Germans, the Dutch, the British, the French, and the Swiss. Certain specific questions will come up—for example, questions about emotions, more in one particular community than in another. But because of global communications, the world is getting smaller, and everybody shares the same concerns—for example, at the moment world peace and health are on everybody's minds.

One of the reasons for my question is that, in my experience, I notice that Buddhists have a tendency or a history of being able to go into very different cultures and merge with the culture. It seems that culture has a lot to do with how one pursues a spiritual path. We all have our cultural baggage. I mean, if we're born here in the United States, we have certain conditioning that we've gone through, certain experiences that we've gone through that someone who was born and raised in England hasn't gone through. They have a different cultural experience. I'm wondering how that cultural experience can become a weight or a baggage in pursuit of one's spiritual path, how you see that affecting one's spiritual pursuit?

Yes, that's an interesting point. I think that if Buddhism does have this ability to blend with different cultures, it's because it is so universal. It deals with understanding the mind, and the deeper nature of life and death. The teachings are so vast and profound, but they are based on facts, on truth and experience, not on a dogma. So, as people discover the teachings for themselves, even the concept of "Buddh-ism" tends to fall away; sometimes I'm not even consciously aware I'm a Buddhist at all. So, it seems that's why it adapts so easily: It is universal like the air we breathe, or the water that's in everything we drink. But at the same time, you're right, I do notice that there are certain patterns or blockages, certain ways of seeing, or a particular sense of humor, that different cultures have developed.

So what would you say would be the typical or common blockages that you encounter in America?

I think that one of the big problems in America is that people display a lot of enthusiasm and energy, but then they "gas out": They just run out of gas. So many things are happening, and so fast; even in the spiritual world—one teacher comes on one weekend, another the next. And there's a constant fascination with the new: Some new Lama comes to town, gives a new set of initiations, and then he goes away again, but there's no follow-up, and people just receive a lot of things, and pile them all up. Only a few individuals actually stay with teachers and really practice. I admire those who do stick to it and keep practicing, because it shows real dedication, particularly in such a speedy environment.

But most of us are so easily swayed by circumstances, particularly when we may not be so clear ourselves, and we have a lot of confusion. What saddens me most is to see people who have been practicing the Dharma for a long time, yet even after a number of years, because they don't change and only go on in the same old way, they end up getting sidetracked, giving up altogether, and falling back into "the ocean of samsara."

One of the great Tibetan masters, Gampopa, the disciple of Milarepa, put his finger on it when he outlined the whole spiritual journey as four "Dharmas," or themes:

"Grant your blessing so that my mind may turn toward the Dharma (the truth);

"Grant your blessing so that the Dharma may become successful in my life;

"Grant your blessing so that the path and practice may clarify confusion;

"Grant your blessing so that confusion may dawn as wisdom."

What can we understand by this? First, it's reflecting and contemplating on our own suffering that gives us the renunciation we need to inspire us to seek the truth of our own nature. But then it is one thing to be interested in Dharma, and quite another to make it really an **integral** part of our lives. This is the vital factor—integration—which so often eludes people on the spiritual path. Next, even if we do succeed in making Dharma part of our life, is our practice able to "clarify confusion"? However powerful the teachings might be, it could be that the way we are practicing them is simply not powerful enough to remove the obstacles that we'll encounter. Finally, with our mind turned toward the Dharma, and having made it successful in our lives, our confusion is actually clarified, so that ultimately it dawns as wisdom.

One of the most important qualities on our spiritual journey is endurance and stability—to keep on practicing. Milarepa said: "Don't entertain hopes of realization, but practice all your life." When you drive from here to Los Angeles, you don't have to keep checking: "Is this the road to L.A.?" As long as you are on the right highway, you don't need to look for signs saying Los Angeles every few miles: you can relax, and be sure that, if you only wait, after a few hours, you'll get to L.A. So we just keep on practicing, in the knowledge that, after a while, we will definitely get somewhere.

Americans have so many wonderful qualities, and perhaps their greatest is their good heart. But the trouble is that, the way their lives are, they are constantly in a hurry. There are so many new things coming out, you're always chasing after something in order to catch up, and as soon as you've got it, then the next thing is happening, and you rush after that. Look at the situation in

Washington: even the name of this week's hot cause will be forgotten next week. So all the time you are running after something, you are never able to rest, and you lose all perspective. It's ironic how many "important" things there are that steal and waste our lives.

So we need to be intelligent and discerning as well. Because along with that good heart, people are also often sentimental, naive, gullible, and easily influenced. It's with the insight that comes from meditation that we can begin to sort out our **real** priorities, and remember the truly important things, which will be the real, deep, human values. When we forget, it's those most important priorities that are completely overlooked. That's often the problem with "progress"; everything is externalized, so there are lots of projections, and we become extremely superficial, obsessed only with the facade and the appearance of things.

You mentioned, in the process of talking, the difficulty of running out of gas, and it brings up the aspect of consistency. We have a term called burnout—*the result of someone actually being consistent and hanging onto something and then burning out on it. How does one avoid the burnout?*

I don't think that burnout is really a problem of consistency. It's when you become obsessive, like a workaholic. It's when you're unskillful, and you lose your sense of meaning and motivation. It's when you don't know how to inspire or nourish yourself. When people get involved with spiritual things, there's a tendency to think and speculate a lot, to look at it constantly this way or that, to see whether they are doing it right or wrong, but without the basic knowledge of Dharma, it's like giving a compulsive worrier something extra to worry about, or an inveterate ditherer the task of making a vital decision. Instead of practicing, people sometimes only wonder about things in their minds, or they imagine that being busy in their minds **is** spirituality, whereas all it is, in fact, is simple confusion. So nothing much gets accomplished on a real level, and people "burn out." Sometimes we need to take a break from all that.

Rinpoche, you were talking about mind-chatter, and how we need to take a break. What causes burnout?

You see, to start with, we don't have a strong grounding in the teachings, and we have our own confusion anyway, and these two are enough on their own to bewilder us and land us in a mess. But on top of that, we are unable to integrate the teachings into our lives, or see any "results," and all we do is indulge in all kinds of expectations, which don't measure up to reality. We can't quite get it, but we don't understand why not. We feel like someone struggling to chew a meal after a dental anaesthetic.

So when people burn out, it's not necessarily because they've been doing a lot of spiritual practice, but often because they've just been doing too much obsessive thinking, and they are not skillful enough to "clarify confusion while on the path." So instead of confusion being transformed into wisdom, it just becomes more confusion! I think this is what happens a lot of the time.

We need to remember that Dharma accomplishes two purposes: it minimizes the ego and brings us the wisdom of discernment. Ego can become the arch-manipulator in proliferating confusion. But when we have less ego and more knowledge, more Dharma, then we can, at the very least, tell what is confusion and what is clarity. Otherwise, when we're confused, we can't even discern one from the other.

I'm wondering about those of us in the West who've been really trained in the mind. The mind has been given an almost supreme position. You go through 12 years of one school. If you go to college, it's four more. If you go to post-graduate school, it's probably three or four more years. You could go to school for

20 years here. It's a lot of emphasis on the mind and thinking. Scientists have shown that the brain has two hemispheres. One side deals with linear, logical thinking, and our educational system is based on essentially one-half of the brain. This other half—the intuitive, the nonlinear—is almost forgotten. With an emphasis like that in a culture like we have in the West, how does one stop thinking? How does one do that? It seems like it's doubly hard compared with the East, where there may be less emphasis on the thinking mind.

It's true that in the modern world the mind is overeducated, but it seems that the mind is trained in a particular way: to ask questions without being ready to hear the answers. There is not the ground of understanding, a culture of wisdom, of nonthinking, of learning simply "to be." Everything, including mind, is accelerated, in the name of progress and activity. This is why everyone yearns to go back to nature, to return to sanity, to find some calm. Everyone's searching for this. What we need is to let the superficial, thinking mind dissolve, so that a deeper aspect of our intelligence is given a chance to manifest. Look at how nourished and enriched we feel whenever we do feel something that inspires or evokes this deeper nature.

This is one of the reasons, I feel, why people have turned to the Dharma, because it offers this simple wisdom, the wisdom of ordinariness, and not only that, but a whole methodology, an unbroken lineage of how to realize it, and, finally, how to be really happy. It has preserved that direct, unbroken lineage of knowledge and wisdom, the real know-how born of experience. The West has spent the last 200 years perfecting material technology. In Tibet, for 12 centuries, in the hermitages and monasteries that were the laboratories of the mind, a spiritual technology was perfected, every bit as precise and rigorous as the disciplines of science.

When you talk about the East, I think one thing you really notice there is that the whole way they look at **emotions** is different. In the West, everything is done to provoke and stir up people's emotions, without a qualm or care for the consequences, but just for the fun of it, or to make money. Each movie has to be more violent than the last in order to grab our attention. Whereas when you go to a country like India, it's far from being perfect, but still you feel very different there emotionally, more calm, more soothed. It's not so highly charged.

So what about the thinking mind? The masters say that what counts most is our **attitude** toward our thinking. They tell us simply to observe the risings, if we can, without reacting to them, but letting them rise and settle, naturally, of their own accord. There's an ancient saying of the masters of Mahamudra and Dzogpachenpo, one which I find so profound and revealing: "If the mind is not contrived, it is spontaneously blissful, just as water, when not agitated, is by nature transparent and clear."

There was something you said once: that it's not the thoughts that matter, it's the thinking of the thoughts.

Yes, my master Jamyang Khyentse Chökyi Lodrö said this in his heart advice to one of his woman disciples:

Body—free of sitting, movement—remain.

Speech—natural to the flow of breath—remain.

Mind—**free of afterthoughts**—remain...

It's not the thoughts or the thinking that delude us, but the **thinking** about **the thoughts**, or the **afterthoughts**. The great master Tilopa said: "It's not appearances that ensnare us; it is our attachment to them...."

You see, the Buddhist teachings are a complete training, one which teaches us how to work with the mind and its thoughts and projections. Because they show us how to deal with the mind's risings, they also show us what the nature of those risings is, and the nature of mind, beyond all the risings. To realize the nature of mind is why we follow a teacher or a teaching. When mind has run so wild, it will take some time to ground ourselves. But then, gradually, we'll see the progress that we are making, and after a while we'll even be able to realize the nature of the risings. Thoughts keep rising as before, but our attitude toward them will be different.

What if the thoughts that come up are angry thoughts or negative emotions? What do we do with those?

Well, there are so many approaches and ways of dealing with them. First of all, we try not to panic, or react with all our normal reactions, and get alarmed. Thoughts are our family, so it's quite natural for us to get angry, as natural as it is for the ocean to have waves, or for a dog to bark! And when we know that negative thoughts are part of our being, no stranger than the waves in the sea, it is that much easier not to be carried away by them.

Then, as we saw earlier, with the practice of meditation, the anger and harm in us are naturally defused, and as the clouds of thought and emotion part and dissolve, a tremendous love is revealed and released. We realize the compassion we have within us, that good heart that will enable us to transform anger into love, and this is the source and basis of the practices of compassion. As the Buddha said, "Anger cannot be destroyed by anger, but by love alone. This is the ancient and eternal law."

One of the ways of transmuting troublesome thoughts and emotions that is used a lot in the Tibetan tradition is mantra. Mantra is defined as "that which protects the mind," in other words, that which protects our mind from its own negativity, from its negative risings. So when our thoughts keep churning and rising, if we keep saying the mantra, slowly its power and the energy will work on our thought processes, and the mind will calm down. Mantra is often used in the case of people who are very nervous or who have lots of uncontrollable thoughts. It can be a very powerful way of directly entering into the state of meditation.

Then, there is the more analytical approach, in which you use that great human gift of reasoning to see where these thoughts are rising from. If anger rises, why is it rising? Does it have any basis in logic or reason? Why should we get angry? You really reason it out and try to get to the root of it and remedy it.

Finally, another way of dealing with angry thoughts and negative emotions is more from an ultimate point of view. This is much more difficult, because first of all you need a good basis of stability in your meditation practice, to keep you on the ground when emotions wash over you. What you do is this: When an emotion arises, you just look directly into it, and it dissolves.

You look straight into the anger. And what happens? What is anger? A state of mind. An emotion. It's in the mind. The one who's looking is also the mind. If the one who is looking directly into the anger is stronger, then anger is less present, since both are mind.

So, if you realize the nature of mind, the view of Shunyata, then whenever emotions arise, it suddenly awakens you. Because the moment you have started to experience negative emotions, you have already been distracted. Distraction reminds you of the view: it becomes an automatic reflex, and the negative emotions become the awakener of wisdom. That very instant you suddenly awaken to the nature of mind is like shining a light into darkness; it dissolves the very instant the light is shone. Because light and darkness simply cannot coexist. So in the light of the nature of mind, anger cannot coexist; it is cut through from its very roots. And as anger is the basis of dualistic grasping—it's our strongest negative emotion—when it is cut through, dualistic grasping itself is liberated there and then. That's more the approach of Vajrayana.

In the practice of Dzogchen, all risings are seen in their true nature, not separate from Rigpa, but as its self-radiance, the manifestation of its very energy. The practitioner maintains the flow of the View of Rigpa, and sees through the risings to what they really are. So even the most turbulent emotions fail to seize hold of him or her, and dissolve like waves back into the ocean, and are liberated. This is how in Dzogchen, an experienced practitioner, can actually use violent emotion to deepen and invigorate the Rigpa; the stronger and more flaming the emotion, the more Rigpa is strengthened.

But you must have a very stable realization of the nature of mind in order actually to "liberate" thoughts when they arise, particularly powerful thoughts and emotions such as anger and desire. It's easy to describe, but very difficult to do, and only comes after years of listening, contemplating, reflecting, meditation, and sustained practice.

We need to build up to this slowly. We need some sort of relative practice first to soften these strong thoughts and emotions, and then come to look at them from an ultimate point of view. And at every point, we need to take to heart deeply what my master Dilgo Khyentse Rinpoche wrote in this wonderful verse:

> Mind is the creator of both samsara and nirvana,
> There is nothing to it: just thoughts and emotions.
> Once we recognize that thoughts are empty,
> Mind will no longer have the power to deceive us.

You know, in some ways Buddhism is a teaching and practice that tends to deal a lot with the human psyche and the human mind, as contrasted with other religions. I'm wondering what you see as the relevance or the contribution that Buddhism can make today to, say, Western psychotherapy or Western psychology.

You're right, the mind is central; in fact, Buddha once summarized his whole teaching:

Commit not a single unwholesome action,
Cultivate a wealth of virtue,
Tame, or train, or subjugate, this mind of ours:
This is the Buddhadharma.

To refrain from harm, to do as much good as possible, and to tame or understand the mind: This is the teaching of Buddha, in three lines. But then when you look at what it is that does harm or good, you see that it's the mind. Mind is the root of everything, the "universal ordering principle', what we call in Tibetan *Kunjé Gyalpo*—'the king who is responsible for everything." Which is why in Buddhism there's such a wealth of knowledge and literature, like the Abhidharma, on mind and psychology.

I think that Buddhism is already making a contribution—that's evident. So many people these days are turning toward Buddhist psychology; I think of the Transpersonal Psychology movement, for example. Of course, if you are looking for them, there are big differences between modern psychology and spirituality: for one thing, spirituality works deeply, to affect many lifetimes, whereas psychology works more with the present-day mind. One speaks of the ground, the other of the risings. One works more on an ultimate and fundamental level, the other deals more with our temporary nature. But on the other hand, if you understand the psyche of a person in terms of spiritual understanding, psychology and Buddhism go naturally hand in hand.

One perspective I find very helpful is that of Thich Nhat Hanh, who speaks of "watering the seeds of joy." From a Buddhist point of view, in our fundamental consciousness, the "alaya," the seeds of experience, of joy and happiness, suffering, pain, anger, and sadness, are all laid down, including impressions from when we were very young. Each time we repeat those experiences, we make them stronger and stronger. So the teaching invites us to water "the seeds of joy," really to enhance and strengthen the positive side of our being, rather than to cultivate the "seeds of pain." In fact, we ignore the negative side by not giving it any importance or too much attention. It's not as if we are neglecting it, or ignoring it altogether; this ignoring is a skillful means. We make sure our positive side becomes steadily stronger, and once we are healthy and strong, then we can look at our negative side.

Of course, one crucial question is whether you know how to relate the Buddhist teachings so that they become therapeutic. Because over 20 years of teaching, what I have come to recognize is that these teachings **are** actually therapeutic, but as they are not taught or understood therapeutically, people think that they're exclusively "spiritual" and don't realize their therapeutic value. Frankly speaking, it's very difficult to make distinctions, because if spiritual teachings work, they **are** therapeutic in their nature, in other words, healing. And one thing that's clear is that when these teachings are directed therapeutically, they can have a very deep effect. One example that interests me more and more is the way that the teaching on compassion can be applied therapeutically, to work deeply with emotions, and so help relieve different kinds of problems of the mind.

These days, we experience so much emotional and psychological fragmentation, and to transmit the Dharma in the West so that it becomes truly a skillful means, I feel it is important to do so in the context of psychology. Buddhism, after all, is a **complete** path to enlightenment, and that includes Western people, and it includes therapy. Therapeutic understanding can help us toward another understanding of the teachings, and when we know what therapy really is, we can discover it, there already, in the Dharma.

EPILOGUE

I first met Sogyal Rinpoche in 1980 and was struck by his ability to communicate difficult spiritual concepts in plain, everyday, practical English. It seemed remarkable to me, given the fact that his native language was Tibetan. Over the years since, he has become even more articulate and is, perhaps, the most important contemporary translator of the rich Tibetan Buddhist traditions in the West. His book, *The Tibetan Book of Living and Dying*, has sold nearly one million copies and has been translated into 25 languages, including Tibetan!

Here in this chapter he has provided some profound advice about how the mind works and why it is important to train the mind, or perhaps I should say, retrain the mind. For those of us who live busy and engaged lives, the principles that Sogyal imparts are like pure cold water to a thirsty traveler in the desert. You don't have to become Buddhist to get value from the teachings. This wisdom has emerged from 2,500 years of practice, practice, and more practice. It's there to benefit everyone.

CHAPTER FOUR

THE WAY OF MINDFULNESS

Jack Kornfield, with Michael Toms

PROLOGUE

*T*here is a spiritual hunger alive in the land. You won't read
about it in the New York Times *or see it portrayed on the
evening news. However, this does not mean that the reality does
not exist. Indeed, in small communities and large cities; rural,
urban, and suburban areas—wherever you go in this land—people are seeking something deeper. Something more real than the
falseness that permeates most modern contemporary life. One of
those traditions that has come to the West and is filling the void
for many Americans is Buddhism.*

*Jack Kornfield is one of those pioneers who has brought
Buddhism into American life over the past two decades. Jack*

was educated at Dartmouth, worked in public health with the Peace Corps in Asia, and has a doctorate in psychology. He was ordained as a Buddhist monk and has taught meditation retreats for the past 20 years in all parts of the United States and Europe. His books include Seeking the Heart of Wisdom; Stories of the Spirit, Stories of the Heart; *and* A Path with Heart: A Guide Through the Perils and Promises of Spiritual Life.

MICHAEL TOMS: Jack, I want to go back to your initial contact with Buddhism and how that occurred. Can you tell us that story?

JACK KORNFIELD: I come from an East Coast scientific and intellectual household, a family of four boys. My father was a scientist who developed artificial hearts and then began in the field of space medicine. Through my family life, I met people who were well educated and successful, and still many of these people were not happy at all. Because my own family life was emotionally very painful, I began to sense that there was something missing, more to life than the scientific and intellectual aspects of the mind. Someone gave me a book on Buddhism, and I was entranced by it, I think because it touched an intuitive place in me that we all have, which one could call our Buddha nature. Somehow each of us knows that there's a potential for greater compassion in our life, and greater awakening. That is really what we long for. That's the source of our happiness. So I was touched in that way. As you recited in my brief biography, I started in premedicine at Dartmouth college and then switched to a major in Chinese and Asian studies. On graduation, I asked the Peace Corps to send me to a Buddhist country so I could ordain in a monastery.

Then you were ordained and spent a number of years in Asia as a monk?

Yes, that's correct. Living as a monk, we had begging bowls and would go out every day, walking across the rice patties to villages where people would wait for us. It wasn't really begging, it was a way of expressing the spiritual life. To offer food to a monk in the morning is a way of honoring the possibility of enlightenment in all beings. It was like a sacred dance to go through the villages as people would bow to you and offer the best of their food. You weren't allowed to say anything; you had to remain silent. All that you could do was receive it—sometimes from very poor people, and realize that it was an honor. To respect that honor you had to live your life with great integrity, so it inspired your practice. I lived for some months initially in a forest monastery, then went to live in a cave monastery, and then back into another forest monastery. Then to Burma over a series of years. I did long meditation retreats and followed the traditional practices, including sitting in the funeral grounds all night long in the forest (as they would bring bodies in to be ceremonially burned), contemplating the cycles of nature, birth, and death.

How was that—coming from a Western background and finding yourself in the jungle and caves?

At first it was very romantic. It was quite a fantastic thing to do. Imagine being a young man, a teenager interested in Buddhism, then learning Chinese and Asian studies in college and Thai and Lao in the Peace Corps. Then I entered a monastery where I was the only Westerner, following a way of life thousands of years old. It was inspiring and very moving. Sometimes very lonely. There are people whom I wanted to tell what was going on, and yet there was no one from my own culture that I could speak to. A good part of the meditation was simply starting to face myself and see my own longing and loneliness and fear and love. Being able to sit with all of that at night in the middle of the forest and make my peace with it. In all, being a monk changed me in many deep ways. My life turned around from it.

You had a teacher who later became famous. Can you tell us about him?

His name was Achaan Chaa. He was not well known when I met him, but in 1993 the king and queen of Thailand and over a million people came to pay their respects at his funeral. He was a humorous, happy, insightful man who also had the greatest sense of peace of anyone I've ever met. You would come and sit in his presence, and he would look at you as if he could look right into you. Then he would laugh, and the laugh would just put you at ease. Whatever you were doing, he'd say, "Oh, you've come a long way. Did you come looking for something?" He would kind of bait you a little bit and then laugh again. He had a way of speaking the truth that everyone could hear very simply. Inviting you to speak back from your heart.

How did you find your teacher?

I was in the Peace Corps visiting monasteries in my area, looking for teachings. I heard that there was a Western man ordained as a monk. I climbed a mountain to an ancient Cambodian temple, and there was an American man who had been in the Peace Corps in Malaysia, sitting on the deck of this tiny, rickety cottage in the Cambodian ruins covered with bees. I walked up to him, and I kind of paid my respects. I said hello. His monk's name turned out to be Achaan Sumedho.

I said, "What's with the bees?" He said, "Well, I came to live up here at this cottage in the Cambodian temple to have a little time to meditate in these ruins. When I moved into this one small hut, I discovered there was a beehive near the roof. At first I kept brushing them off, being frightened they'd sting me. Then I realized that it was their hut as much as mine and that they could have the top and I could use the bottom, and we kind of made our peace with one another. So now we share this hut."

I knew I'd met a very unusual person. He told me about a teacher he had just met that year whom he found to be enormously inspiring—in part because he wasn't treated special as a Western monk. He said, "This teacher made me do all the difficult things everyone else had to do in training, and that's what I was longing for—to really be respected as a practitioner." So on his recommendation, I went the next month and met my teacher, Achaan Chaa. That American monk now has become the abbot of six monasteries in England. He's been ordained for 25 years and was just honored by the king of Thailand and made a "bishop" in the Buddhist hierarchy—the first Westerner in Southeast Asia to be really esteemed as a genuine meditation master and abbot within his own tradition.

Then you came back to the United States, and that was a bit of a transition, wasn't it?

It was quite a culture shock. I came back in robes. In 1972, I wanted my family and friends to see what I'd been doing and to somehow connect the two worlds. I lived with my parents in Washington, D.C., for some time because there weren't any Buddhist monasteries to go into. Then I decided to visit my twin brother in New York. So my mother got me a train ticket. I wasn't using money. I was barefoot, and I had my begging bowl.

That was part of the tradition, not to use money?

Part of the vows of the monk was to live simply with only your bowl and your robes and show your faith in a sacred and simple way of life. If you lived in a worthy way, it was hoped you would be taken care of, and I was. People fed me. So then I was given a ticket and put on the train to New York. I was to meet my twin brother's wife, Tori. She had just had a birthday, and for a gift, my twin brother gave her a certificate for a day at Elizabeth Arden's in New York. A massage, a facial, a manicure, and hairdo. It sounds quite pleasant.

I was to meet her at the end of that day, and the train came into Grand Central Station. I got out and I began to walk up Fifth Avenue. I was still somewhat in the consciousness of the forests of Thailand and Burma after many years. So I was barefoot, and the cars were going by, and there was Tiffany's and all the people. I felt absolutely peaceful. Walking meditation up Fifth avenue, with the same inner peace as the monastery. I got to the corner of Elizabeth Arden's, and she didn't come out. I waited patiently, and finally thinking I was there at the wrong time or something, I went in and the receptionist was shocked. What are you doing here? Can I help you? I guess they don't get a lot of Buddhist monks in Elizabeth Arden's. So I said, "I'm waiting for Mrs. Kornfield," and she said, "Oh, she's not finished yet. There's a waiting lounge. Please go to the fourth floor."

I took the elevator, and the receptionist there was equally shocked. She said, "Well, please take a seat." So I sat down on the bench and was just waiting. There wasn't much else to do, so being a Buddhist monk, I folded my legs and I started to meditate. Close my eyes. Feel my breath, and just center myself. After about five minutes, I hear all these voices. I look around. What's going on, you know? And one of these voices yells out quite loud, "Is he for real?" So my eyes open wide, and I look, and in front of me are a dozen women wearing what look like Elizabeth Arden nighties. These are a kind of smocks you wear for the day. There were women with their hair in curlers and mud on their face. Or avocado smeared all on them or these fishing-rod contraptions to curl their hair, and I looked back. I thought I was on some other planet. Then I said, "Are *they* for real?" Somehow in that moment I recognized that I had to find a way to integrate the wonderful teachings of the monastery back into modern Western culture. That's what I've tried to do as a student and as a teacher over the last 20 years.

Since we are brought up in the West, we sometimes think that once we get on a spiritual path, everything will be hunky-dory-rosy, that we'll get along okay, and all the problems will disappear. How is it? Is that the way it works?

Well, that was my own notion as well. I think we were all kind of romantic and idealistic. Hearing about Tibet and the stories of great lamas and Zen masters. But it turns out that the journey is much more what Chögyam Trungpa portrayed as manual labor. My own journey has been downward. I did ten years of study and practice in meditation—opening my mind, with insights, visions, dissolving my body into light. Then, when I came back from the monastery, I had many tests for that wonderful training. I got back and went to graduate school and got into a relationship with a woman. I lived with her and her two children. Alas, high as I'd been, I fell as low. I found all my old habits were there waiting for me to put on like old clothes.

In some way, I had used spiritual life to learn new things, but also to run away, to escape. When I came back, the habits happened again. The horror of it was that I could see it all the more clearly. I couldn't close my eyes anymore. Ram Dass says that at some point you become a connoisseur of your neurosis. I saw the fears and the loneliness and the kind of things that had gotten me into great difficulty before re-arising. So I began to work my way down from the mind to the heart. I realized that practice must be centered in the heart, not just visions and understanding. I began to do a lot of work with compassion and lovingkindness meditations. The whole way that I practiced and taught changed. Initially, I saw spiritual practice as entering the great spiritual realms, and later I saw that the realms were simply to inform us so that we might return to our lover, our neighbor, the way we eat and drive and bring to that tremendous compassion.

Once several years ago I had the opportunity to visit with his Holiness, the Dalai Lama in India. I was working on a show for National Public Radio where we interviewed teachers on spirituality and social responsibility. My wife and I and two journalists visited the Dalai Lama. After the splendid interview, we were all sitting there grinning, because he also served us tea. He was so gracious. Finally, it was done, and he said, "Don't you want to take my picture?" We all had our cameras, but we were so excited being with him that we'd forgotten that. So he said, "Give your cameras to the attendant, and we'll take the pictures, and we can be in it together."

So we took pictures, and then he held my hand and turned to me, knowing that I was a Buddhist teacher. He'd been to the Buddhist center we founded in Massachusetts, and had given teachings. I expected he was going to ask me how teaching was going. You know, how's business? Because we work for the same company. But he didn't. He looked at me very carefully, and then said, "You're so skinny. You should eat more!" That was the blessing of the Dalai Lama.

Somehow all the spiritual states that we might attain only become useful when they're translated into how we care for our bodies, our lovers, and the earth around us. Our gardens. Our communities. Our neighbors. This is a maturing that I see among many of us, that spiritual life that is not a journey out to someplace else. It is finding what the Buddha discovered, a greatness of heart that can sit in the midst of all things with compassion and with ease. That's what meditation is about.

We live in a culture, a society, that's so fast-paced that we're surrounded by distractions of extraordinary variety and diversity. How does one go about removing one's self or separating one's self from all these distractions that are there to capture us at every moment?

There are two kinds of stillness. There's the stillness that comes when we remove our self from the business of modern society, and at times we need that as much as we need sleep. Just as there are times that our body just has to sleep, we also need to rest our hearts, walk in the mountains, go to the ocean, take a little time just to put our feet up on the coffee table and breathe and not turn the news on. Sometimes I think the greatest political act you can do is to turn off CNN and turn on Mozart. Some days you really need to get in touch with the natural rhythm of your breath and see what stage the leaves are on the trees out your window. Part of us requires periods of stillness, and nature or meditation offers that. There's another kind of stillness, and this is even more central to the awakening of the Buddha, to anyone who awakens their own Buddha nature. Maybe I should tell a little story to illustrate that.

Pope John the 23rd (this is true) said that sometimes it happens that, "I wake up at night when there's a very difficult problem I'm wrestling with. I struggle with it, and then I think, I must go and talk to the Pope about it. Then I wake up more fully, and I remember I *am* the Pope." This is a bit like meditation. We sit to remember we are the Buddha. Our own Buddha nature is here in any moment. This second kind of stillness is called stillness in the midst of activity. It is the still point, the centeredness, that we may find first by walking in the mountains or sitting in meditation and breathing quietly. There we can reconnect with it, but then it's possible to have it in the midst of our life. If we feel our breathing. If we feel each step as we walk. If we remember to come back to our hearts and to feel what we most deeply value in ourselves.

This is where Eastern practice and our Western life fit together. How do we live it with our neighbors? Or when we drive on the highway? Can we make that a part of our meditation? You can with some practice. Even if you're driving in your car, you can feel the weight of your body in the seat of the automobile. You can feel your hands on the wheel. If you're sitting at home in a chair, you can feel the fact that your body breathes itself. There's this natural, wonderful rhythm of breathing, and you can trust your breath. You can trust the seat of the car and the earth to hold you. You can relax a little—maybe move out of the high-speed lane, over one lane.

Would you like to give our readers an example of a guided meditation?

This is a sample meditation that can take just take two or three minutes. The truth of meditation is that it is a simple practice. It's a practice of *being* rather than *doing* anything. We're such a *doing* culture. You can have someone read this to you while you listen:

> Feel yourself wherever you are. Whether it's driving or perhaps, more suitably, sitting in a chair or sitting somewhere listening. First of all, become aware of your own body. As you feel your own human body, sense the warmth or the coldness—the areas of tension or tightness that you hold within yourself. As you feel it, begin to relax. Let your shoulders relax. Let your eyes and face be soft, and let your jaw relax. Let your breathing become soft and natural—relaxed, and yet present and alert.
>
> Usually we only relax when we go to sleep, but here, feel a relaxation and a presence. Let your heart be soft, as well, to receive whatever is arising in this moment with compassion, with kindness. As you relax and feel your body, notice that there are sounds—these words you hear. Sensations—the areas of tension, perhaps. Even the wounds or places of hurt you carry or any illness in your body. The unfinished business, the dreams, the thoughts that arise. Let them come and go like the waves of the ocean. Allow yourself to rest as if on a boat that can float safely and comfortably rocked by the waves. Sounds come and go. Sensations arise in your body. Let them soften.
>
> In the midst of all these, be aware of the fact that you're

breathing. Feel your life breath. Even if it's very soft, feel how the breath breathes itself in a natural way. Rest in that gentle movement of breathing as you drive or sit or hear other things, knowing that you can find a stillness in the midst of the other activities. Rest in that place. Let the waves come and go. You don't have to do or change anything. When your mind wanders away, which it will, that's fine. Simply notice that the mind has wandered off, and when you're aware, come back gently, directly, to feel the next breath. Notice what's present. Is there happiness? Longing? Pain? Sorrow? Joy? Excitement? To meditate is listening. Looking in the mirror. Hold whatever is present with compassion, with great kindness. The very compassion and attention will allow it to teach you. Will allow it to release or change. Will bring you back to that which is your true nature. Will let you rest.

What about the truth of the illusion about meditation taking us away from life? Taking us out of life somehow. That we're going to disappear into a cloud or whatever, and we're not really going to embrace life and its challenges. What does meditation have to do with taking care of the problems that we have around us? What is your answer to that?

It's a very important question. We in the West have managed to misuse or abuse many things. We have exploited the environment and one another and often misused the gifts of science and technology. So there's no reason that we won't also at times misuse meditation and spiritual life. It is a misuse and a misunderstanding of meditation and spiritual life to think that it is an escape. Such false spirituality is based on fear and confusion and aversion. There is no such thing as a spiritual end run or bypass. The enemy of true equanimity, the great wisdom of a Buddha, is a state that appears like it but is really different, and that's called indifference. Indifference is the way to run away, to escape.

Genuine meditation is different. Imagine if there's a room,

and you take a chair and you place it in the center of that room and you sit down on it. You open the doors and windows, which are the doors and windows of your senses, and you let whatever needs to, arise. Your fears. Your longings. Unfinished business. All of that is your meditation. So, the first step of meditation is to actually be with yourself. Many of us don't know how to do that. We spend our lives turning on the TV, being addicted to various substances, calling on the telephone. Anything but feeling bored or lonely or longing for the other things within us. So, the first step of meditation is, in a sense, to confront yourself and find that deep place of compassion where you can be at home with yourself. That's like breathing in. Then the next breath is to get up and extend it into the world around you.

In Zen they say there are only two things: "You sit and you sweep the garden, and it doesn't matter how big the garden is." That is, first you find some peace in yourself. If we can't do it, the world will be in bad shape. It's a grave political necessity that someone find peace in the midst of their own franticness, fear, greed, or hatred because these are the forces that fuel war and create starvation in one place while grain elevators are full of food in another. Until we can face our own greed, desire, fear, and hatred, we can't really help the world. If the inbreath is to sit and make our peace by really facing these great forces, then the outbreath is to get up and sweep the garden. It is to offer our peaceful heart to our families and our communities through parenting, politics, economics, or art, whatever way brings our gift into the world.

There's this term you used called "engaged Buddhism." *Can you give us the definition of that term.* Engaged Buddhism, *what does it mean?*

Engaged Buddhism is Buddhist practice engaged in bringing compassion to the problems of the world. The Buddha discovered the central truth that we are not independent but interdependent. So when you become still in meditation and feel your own breath or body, you realize that your body is made up of the water and the clouds and the air around you. You experience that you're completed interconnected. And in feeling that interconnection, then you can't only sit on your cushion or retire to some far-off monastery and live there isolated. You discover that what you do, and what your meditation is, is directly connected with all beings. So that your meditation must engage you in the sorrows of the world and the healing of sorrows. There's a big movement that expresses these teachings led by Zen master Thich Nhat Hanh, or his Holiness the Dalai Lama, and many others who follow in the spirit of Gandhi and Martin Luther King, Jr. To bring spiritual life and justice together for all beings is engaged Buddhism.

It is also the work of Robert Aitken Roshi.

Yes. He's a wonderful teacher. In this spirit, there's a poem I want to recite, a short one by David Budbill called *Bugs in a Bowl*. Hanshan, that great crazy wonder-filled Chinese poet of a thousand years ago, said:

We're just like bugs in a bowl.
All day going around
And never leaving their bowl. I say that's right.
Every day climbing up the steep sides, sliding back
    over and over again,
Up and back down.
Sit in the bottom of the bowl,
Head in your hands, crying, moaning,
Feeling sorry for yourself.
Or look around.
See your fellow bugs walking around.
Say, hi, how are you doing?
Say, nice bowl.

There's some way in which we take our spiritual life too seriously if we think it means to go and hide. If it doesn't bring you greater compassion and kindness and the capacity to be more open and genuine, more true with yourself and others, then it's not wisdom. It's something else, but it's not really the maturity of the heart. The greatness of your own Buddha nature.

What you're saying does bring up the idea of the ups and downs of the spiritual path. In fact, there's even a chapter in your book A Path with Heart *about that. Again, I think we're conditioned to expect that the spiritual path is going to be nothing but clear sliding, you know, once we're on it. Yet, it's probably the most difficult path to pursue.*

Yes. If we genuinely undertake the spiritual path, we have to go into our shadow as much as into the light and face the very fears and things that we have avoided our whole lives. That's what makes a greatness of heart. Anyone who undertakes a spiritual discipline over time discovers that the mind has no pride. It will do anything. That we contain multitudes, as it's been said. Zen master Hui Neng said, "As far as the Buddha nature is concerned, there is no difference between a sinner and a sage. One enlightened thought and one is a Buddha, and one foolish thought, and one is again an ordinary person." You can see how true that is. You can have great, exalted experiences in one moment, and in another moment be an idiot. What comes from this realization is patience and a certain kind of humility. Not the false humility of, "Oh, I'm a humble person," but really a kindness toward yourself.

I was leading a retreat some years ago, and at the end of this ten-day retreat for a hundred or so people, we were supposed to do a lovingkindness meditation and a ceremony. I was having a fight with my girlfriend at the time on the telephone that morning. She and I were very upset with one another, and then the bell rang and I had to go in, where I had promised I would lead this meditation of opening lovingkindness. So I went in the meditation hall and sat there. The bell rang, and I started to guide a meditation with my softest lovingkindness voice. "Think of someone you love a lot, and extend kindness to them." Then I paused while people could meditate. Then my mind started to get angry and judgmental. "That bitch. What she said is completely unfair. I'm going to call her back. I was so upset. Then I said out loud, "Now think of someone else you love a lot and send your lovingkindness to them." But my mind said, "She has done this for the last time. I'm going to tell her a thing or two." It would alternate between these loving words and angry thoughts. My mind was going back and forth, and I'd done enough meditations so finally I could just sit there and laugh to see the paradox of our human nature. Finally, I came to some forgiveness. Of course, it's fear that is really what most of anger is about. Fear and hurt. There's love, too, and that's what we want. The compassion of the Buddha is to sense that our heart is much greater than all of our reactions and rest in that which is timeless within us.

I recall you saying something one of your teachers told you after a long period of silent meditation and concern, about fear. One of your teachers said something about fear always being with you.

Yes, but it is not a problem. I had a splendid experience of this with Achaan Chaa. We were driving to a little mountain temple on the Cambodian border. It was 80 miles over a one-and-a-half-lane twisty dirt road. We had this rickety Toyota and one of those kind of drivers that you get—I don't know, you can get them in New York or Boston, but certainly in the Third World—who seems intent on dying behind the wheel. Madman passing buses, you know, while going around curves. Speeding blindly between ox carts, logging trucks, and water buffalo and on this narrow road. I was holding on for dear life and breathing. Saying, "Well, I guess I'm going to die as a Buddhist monk." Trying to do my death prayers. Then I looked over, and my teacher's knuckles were as white as mine. Somehow that was reassuring to me. Finally, we got there. We made it. The car stopped, and then Ajahn Chaa turned and looked at me. He smiled, "Scary ride, wasn't it?"

I just laughed, and I breathed. He was a man who I knew was ready to die. In many ways he showed that he was unafraid of death. He was a peaceful person, profoundly centered. In that moment, he simply acknowledged that it was a scary ride, and he laughed. It was as if he simply bowed to it, it was just what it was, with no problem. This perspective was a great gift. In the same way, meditation is a gift. It allows us to honor what is so and hold it with great kindness. It's only with respect and kindness that we can go into our depths. It is only with this same compassion that we can heal the most deeply wounded places in ourselves and that we can bring our wisdom to the great political/economic problems of the world and make a genuine difference.

Buddhism is something that has had this amazing facility of integrating itself into cultures around the world in different parts of the world. As Buddhism comes into America, do you see that there is a kind of an American Buddhism emerging out of traditional Buddhism?

I see the signs of it already. For example, it's quite exciting to see a shift from the traditional Buddhism in Asia that is very hierarchical. In the monasteries, there are masters and assistant masters and sub-assistant masters, and decisions are made from the power structure on down. But we are a much more democratic culture. In the American Buddhist centers, I see a whole shift. People don't just want to follow the teacher blindly. As they mature spiritually, they want to question and understand. Instead of hierarchy, many Buddhist centers are developing councils and boards, senior students who work together with the teachers. This is a new open-minded American flavor. It doesn't mean we're going to vote on the teachings, but it means as Buddhism grows here, we can talk openly and question authority. I think it's enormously healthy, and it's actually helping send a positive message back to Buddhism in Asia.

A second major trend in America is a new feminization of Buddhism. Traditionally, Buddhism was patriarchal and masculine in the deeper sense; it was more to do with the mind and logos—with the warrior spirit and the ideal of overcoming the body through great effort. Yes, there are many more women teachers in the West. But more importantly, the feminine element is bringing a wise relationship to the earth and all of life. In another way, the deep feminine is becoming awakened through Buddhism's connection with the ecology movement and through Buddhism's engagement in the spheres of justice and service that you spoke about. American Buddhism will have more women as abbots and great teachers than anywhere else. And with the feminine is coming a whole change of language.

The Buddha himself was a warrior prince, and he used a samurai-style language for describing the spiritual path.

In Asia, I practiced that way as a young man, as a kind of initiation—sit for 12 hours and don't move. Walk for 24 hours, and then sit 12 hours in the charnel grounds all night. It had its benefits, and I had very powerful experiences, but for many in the West this effortful style of practice ties them in knots. Most Westerners begin with so much self-judgment that they are already in a battle against themselves. What they really need is kindness and not fighting against themselves. The change that I see in Buddhism in the West is that our practice is coming to embrace all, all of life with compassion, to bring awareness to the shadow side of ourselves and see it wisely, rather than fight ourselves in a battle.

The different Buddhist traditions in the West are learning from each other, and even from Western psychology. They are discovering the need to integrate genuine practice into the everyday life of committed lay people. Feminization and integration begin to give us a sense that Buddhism in America will be quite a different animal. In Asia, the practice of meditation was mostly held in monasteries, in the mountains, and in caves by a small group of people. There, laypeople simply go and offer food and hope to make good karma, so that in the next life they'll be a monk or a nun who can practice. In America, people don't want to ordain as monks and nuns, but they want to do the genuine practices heading to enlightenment. They want the awakening that was held in the treasuries of those great monasteries. But here, we are developing a much more integrated practice for householders who say, "Yes, I want to learn to really live an authentic spiritual life, awaken my Buddha nature, but I want to do it as a layperson."

One of the problems that has occurred as Americans have come in touch with traditions and teachings and disciplines from the East—and this is true of Buddhism as well—is that there's a tendency to project onto the teachers our own ideals or whatever. So this has caused some problems in some communities. There's almost a co-dependence, as we understand it, in Western psychology, then we apply it to the spiritual path. We become co-dependent with the teacher or whatever. What about this?

You raised two different questions. One is about co-dependence and compassion. How do they fit together? Somebody said, from one standpoint, Mother Teresa is the ultimate co-dependent, and yet clearly she's not. Clearly there's something else going on. The other is projection, all the ways that we imagine a teacher must be because we have a skewed notion of perfection. We think that a great teacher is going to be perfect according to our ideas. I got so frustrated with my own teacher because he wouldn't act the way I thought a great master should. Sometimes he would sit there and just chat with the villagers, and while he was doing it, he would be scratching himself. I thought, he can't be completely mindful doing that. So I confronted him one day when I was having a hard time in meditation, and I couldn't confront myself. Now I know better.

Anyway, I went and I confronted him instead. I said, "You're not such a great teacher. I'm having a hard time," which I thought was his fault. I said, "Besides which, you know you don't even seem so enlightened to me. You're not consistent. You say one thing and then you say another. You're not acting like you're enlightened to me." He laughed. He thought it was very funny because Asians never would say that. Only a Westerner has that kind of nerve. He said, "You know, it's a really good thing I don't look like the Buddha to you." I said, "Why is that?" I was ready to leave. He said, "Because if I fit your image of the Buddha, you'd still be caught in looking for him outside yourself, and he's not out here. Go back and meditate. If you want to find the Buddha, he's inside. Look to your compassion and not in your ideas."

We've got teachers, lamas, and Zen masters that come to the West, and we imagine they're perfect in every way. They must have perfect personalities and perfect habits. Because I'm sort of in the enlightenment business, I get to know a lot of lamas and Zen masters. I admire them, but they're a terribly eccentric group. They're as weird as anyone else I've ever met. The best of them are very compassionate and very free in certain ways. But we mistake the notion that someone can be kind or wise in one area to imagine it means they're perfect in every other way. People go to meditation teachers and say, "What kind of car should I buy?" or "What kind of labor should I plan for my baby that's coming?"

Some friends asked a young Tibetan lama about labor, but he

knew nothing about childbirth. He said, "Well, in old Tibet, we did it this way." So they went into the mountains and tried it. The baby almost died. A wise teacher can offer inner understanding, kindness, and freedom, but it doesn't mean they know everything. We Americans have had a long, difficult process in sorting that out.

The same thing with co-dependence that you speak about. It's common for people who are gravely wounded or lonely or have histories of abuse to say, "Ah, now I'll go do spiritual practice, and this great master and his practice will heal me." What happens in a spiritual community is that you attract many wounded people or people from backgrounds of painful families. If you get enough of us—I include myself in them—all of a sudden we make a new family, and unfortunately it can turn out that it's not very different from the one we ran away from. As a result, many spiritual communities have the same fears—secrecy, the same tendency toward denial and abuse as our families of origin. Spiritual teachers who have not dealt with that in themselves get sucked in, in the same way. They get very isolated, and they become part of the same dynamic.

The scandals that we see—whether it's Buddhist or Christian television ministers, it doesn't really matter—happen when the teachers themselves get really isolated and believe all these imaginary things that the students project on them. Remember the passage from Hui Neng about the Buddha nature, that there's no difference between a sinner and a sage. We have within us every possibility, and that's part of what's wonderful about a teacher like the Dalai Lama. He says, "Me, too. I have the same difficulties as you. We must do what we can. Be straightforward and honest about it." In that way, the real compassion and real maturity of our hearts, our kindness to one another, awakens, and genuine freedom comes.

I'll tell another story if I may. I was in India in the village of Bodh Gaya, which is a holy place for Buddhists. It's the village that has the tree that the Buddha sat under to be enlightened, or so the story is told. There's a big temple there, and many pilgrims and other temples. My first time in this village, I went to practice for a month-and-a-half in these temples. When I went to the great Mahabodhi temple where the bodhi tree is, outside I passed a long line of beggars. The beggars are there because there are pilgrims. It's a good place to ask for money. So I thought, Oh, here I'm a generous young man.

I didn't have much money, but I went and I started to give the money I could spare to the beggars. They were delighted, and I was too. I felt really happy with myself. But the next day I came, and I didn't have money left. I'd given away what I could. Still the beggars came up, and they wanted more money from me, and they started to follow me to get money. For the whole month, they tried to get money from me because I'd given money to the beggars in the beginning. So next time I said, "All right, I'll do it differently."

The next year when I went, I didn't give. I saved it till the last day, and I got a lot of money, and I was going down the line of beggars, trying to give it to each one respectfully. Very carefully. I got halfway down the row of 150 beggars, and the rest got afraid I was going to run out of money, so 75 beggars ran after me in a huge crowd and started pulling at my clothes and pulling at me. I had to run away and throw the money at them from a distance because I was really frightened. I turned back, and they were on their knees in the dirt picking up this money that I wanted to give to them as an offering, fighting each other. I realized I had a lot to learn about what it means to be skillfully generous. It's not our ideas about it, but there takes a kind of common sense and wisdom as well. I had learned about my own limits. The next time I gave money to the Gandhi ashram, who helped the poorest children in the village. In spiritual life, what matters is not our ideals, but our willingness to be honest and kind over and over. It is not the perfection of ourselves, or of some special state of enlightenment that matters. It is the perfection of our love and patience, of our hearts, goodness and freedom in the midst of all things.

EPILOGUE

The value of Jack Kornfield's insights come from his own hard-earned experience, gathered from years of pursuing his path. There is an engaging quality about his remarks, because he is willing to see himself clearly and share his personal revelations with complete candor. In that way, he is a model for the rest of us to emulate, because mostly we fool ourselves into believing that we are someone else. It is difficult to face our faults and short-comings. However, as he points out, it is only through looking within and seeing ourselves clearly that we can begin to discover who we really are.

Also, the idea of "engaged Buddhism" where we bring our spiritual experience into the everyday world of sorrows, is especially important for the times we live in. It is no longer appropriate to retreat from the world in isolated contemplation on a mountaintop, but rather we must, "bring that gift into the world." The spiritual path is not easy, but it is the only path worth traveling.

CHAPTER FIVE

SPIRITUAL INTELLIGENCE

Marsha Sinetar, with Michael Toms

PROLOGUE

A merican culture emphasizes the material world. Value is often measured in terms of one's possessions. We get caught up in how much we have or don't have. At the same time, more than 80 percent of the 75 million baby boomers consider themselves religious and say they believe in an afterlife. There is this paradox of overt materialism and covert spirituality. How is it possible to follow a spiritual life in these times? The answer to this and other questions about the emergence of the spirit and the care of the soul serves as the focus in this chapter.

Marsha Sinetar is one of the foremost exponents of the spiritual aspects of self-actualization. She is an author, educator, and corporate psychologist with extensive background in both education and management. Her books include Ordinary People as Monks and Mystics; *the classic* Do What You Love, the Money Will Follow; Elegant Choices, Healing Choices; To Build the Life You Want, Create the Work You Love; *and* A Way Without Words: A Guide for Spiritually Emerging Adults.

MICHAEL TOMS: *A good place to begin is at the place where spirituality merges with a materialistic world. This is a paradox—people following the spirit and living in a society that's based on capitalism and material goods. We're all exposed to television commercials and the idea of "Buy more, buy more." How does one follow the spirit in the midst of all that?*

MARSHA SINETAR: Instead of looking at *How* first, I think it's more pertinent to ask, *What?* What is spirituality? If you just take the simplest dictionary definition, it's our animating essence. If you think about animating essence, this is where our vitality, our power, our creative juices come from. Our love/health and focus, so on and so forth—including our ability to influence. If we issue forth that animation and develop it, think of the impact we can have in the material world.

If you look at all the really inspirational leaders—not just my idea, but anyone's idea of an inspirational leader—what you see is animating essences or lively spirituality. Then we can go to *How.* Each person has a little different take on *How,* if animating essence is the goal. This gets us right into it.

Where does meditation fit into that?

Here, again, it is individualized for each person. I happen to be the type of person for whom silence and meditation, reflection, reading of scripture, music—all these things are very important. For that type of person, meditation has its definite place. There are other people who meditate when they move. When they dance, they might experience a kind of sufi kinesthetic prayer. So that's where that comes in. There might be someone else for whom art is the meditation. Like Ben Shahn, the great graphic artist. So you see, you must return to:Who am I as a person? What brings me to life? How can I capture that? How can I honor that? Then everything in your day falls into place. This is what's so beautiful about the spiritual journey.

We've all been conditioned to the idea that we have to have a tradition or a practice or a discipline. What about that?

Tradition lasts for a reason. In other words, it wouldn't last if it weren't valuable. So I make a distinction in some of my writing now. In *A Way Without Words*, for example, I suggest that we have a spirituality that is untidy, idiosyncratic, and generally elusive. Then we have religion or religious and meditative traditions—whatever you'd want to talk about. This seems more linear. We can communicate about it. Religion helps us shape our life and gives voice to that in us which is unique. I have only the greatest respect for these traditions.

I guess the thing is not to put the cart of doctrine before the horse of spirituality. Not to say, "Oh, I'll blindly follow this tradition when it has no real bearing on who I am at heart." Even in the different major religions, for example—Christian or Jewish or Buddhist and so forth—within each body of thought there are avenues that different people can take to express their spirituality. This is a time-honored tradition, if you will. I just say all people are different, and there are as many ways to express one's innermost essence as there are people and techniques in and of themselves.

With the advent of Eastern practices and philosophies coming to the West, there is this idea that one needs a teacher. Where are you with that?

As a Christian, the person of Jesus Christ is available to me; the Comforter or Holy Spirit *is* my teacher. We read this in the Bible. Here, again, I must repeat it's not my vocation, or calling, to convince anybody that I'm right. Rather, I like to discuss these issues because they are important to me. Yet, I have personal friends who have had teachers, who do travel to India to study. For instance, the couple next door have a spiritual teacher—a guru. They live with him, and come back totally revitalized, feeling transformed. My way is different: more traditional. Plus, I seem to have an ascetic, contemplative streak that runs through my work and life.

But you're still saying in your writing that certainly spirituality is very ecumenical. You're basically allowing for all traditions and all practices, as best as I can tell.

Yes. What I'm describing is a condition or state of mind, if you will—God-consciousness, I guess you'd call it. There are so many ways to discuss God-consciousness—and certainly spirituality is a wholly human issue.

It's interesting that in our culture, when you say that word God, then a lot of past experiences come up around that word, around that idea of God. I'm sure it's true with everybody. I can certainly tell in the way some people behave regarding that word that it precludes other experiences. It's as if they think, Oh no, we are going to get into God now. That's a whole other story. That doesn't really relate to life. That's not practical or that's something else. That's on Sunday, or that's another compartment. What about that?

My experience in growing up was so different. As a child, raised in a liberal, intellectual atmosphere, I had sophisticated parents who didn't really want to talk about religious subjects. My grandmother and I were sort of family renegades. We enjoyed going to church and Buddhists temples and so forth. So my experience of God was of this wonderful Friend, you know.

Getting to your point, last week a New York publisher said about a new manuscript, "Marsha, we loved this manuscript, but you've got to get rid of that God-word." He called it the God-word, you know, as if it were an expletive. I don't know what to say about that. The beginning of sanity is to know when we are activated—how we react to different words.

Here again, I don't really have a problem if someone wants to substitute a word. Now I hear Goddess used a lot in the lexicon. You know, in America's public dialogue. I have no problem with the word *God*. I prefer it, and so I use it. Interestingly enough, many people approach me and sort of shyly, on the side, say, "I'd like to talk to you about a spiritual experience I had recently." For example, when a doctor's son was born—this is a man who professes to be an atheist—when his son was born, he looked into his child's face and said, "I had an experience—I guess you'd call it, an experience of God." Now here he sounded nearly derisive, but not really. The more he talked, the more he grew convinced: "I saw not only my son, but all children. That epiphany connected me to some human interconnection, you know, larger than me. Larger than my family or the human family." Of course, this is an essential spiritual experience.

You are pointing out that it's not just God, but it's the whole aspect of spirituality that gets left in the closet. In the last few years, though, we've been seeing this coming up through the concrete, as if little flowers of spirituality were emerging.

That's so true. Spirituality is life, like a little shoot of life coming up. We're spiritually starved. The world is hungry for Reality, capital *R*. All of the materialism that you talked about previously does not nourish us. It's like eating fast food. You know, the aggressive push for power is not at all what our soul needs. But the recollected, innocent heart brings such joy. You can exist much longer without food than you can without that spiritual nourishment, that joy. Even beauty—as Poe noted—is an immortal instinct within our soul. We absolutely need beauty, gratefulness, joy.

One of the things that struck me in A Way Without Words *that I hadn't really thought about but is absolutely true is how we've come to identify what midlife crisis is about, that now it's okay. It's a more positive experience than it was in the fifties. It was real serious a few decades ago. Now it's become more acceptable, and there's a realization that it's moving to something else, another cycle.*

That's right. Probably as we age as a population, we'll gain growing respect for what I call a spiritual moratorium: A time out. We ask: "How much time do I have left? What do I value?" You know, "What are my governing values? How do I live those values in the time that I have left?" In times of fatigue, crisis, transition—more, not less, time out for reflection is spiritually intelligent.

I brought that up because I was thinking of how, as we get older and as we come to that midlife place, we're looking for something deeper. Many of us are looking for something deeper than we've had in our previous cycle of life.

I live on the coast of Northern California, and also now up in Washington. I have many neighbors who are over 70. (I guess you have to be retired to live up where I live. Well, either that or an artist.) The happiest people that I know are not necessarily traditionally religious. But they seem people who have cultivated a spiritual understanding of themselves and their Creator—whatever term you would put to that. They've settled into their place in the largest scheme of things. Perhaps they've invented it. For one reason or another, they don't really fear what's on the other side. They've come to terms with their transitions. Spiritual maturity brings great harmony. I sense others are more brittle. For them, we see old age being a winter of discontent.

So another aspect of this topic is that in the fifties, many people felt that a midlife crisis was when you went out and bought a red Ferrari or a Porsche or whatever. We don't view it that way today. We see it, as you were saying, as a coming to terms with life itself. It's organic, one's changing seasons.

You used a phrase in A Way Without Words—*"spiritual intelligence." What do you mean by spiritual intelligence?*

I mean illumined brightness—in the same way that researchers at Harvard and Yale now say that we have multiple intelligences, not just one way of figuring things out. For example, if you observe children's precociousness, this is the easiest place to see spiritual intelligence (and other sorts, too). There are children who are musically intelligent. They have a good ear, we say. Or physically intelligent—they are our gymnasts. They can do things with their bodies—you know, break-dancing—that we cannot imagine doing. Mathematical brightness is another intelligence. Or verbal ability. Well, in that same way, there are those who are bright in a way that's otherworldly. These are our seers and pathfinders who speak to us of unfamiliar realities. Provided they're sane and can make a connection to us through their communication, we can learn a great deal from such people: They speak our heart's language.

How about faith and hope? Is there a difference between faith and hope?

Hope leads us to faith. For example, I might hope to locate some truth in this or that book and turn to it. Then I find what I am looking for, and now I have faith in that. That's the way I'd slice that difference. Hope is often longing: It turns us in the direction of our aim. Faith is the substance of things unseen, we're taught in Scripture. So in other words, what we usually call faith is positive faith—because we also have fear, which is a negative faith. But with faith, in the provisions of the Bible—let's talk in those terms because that's the way I've interpreted it—we don't actually trust our eyesight. We don't trust our senses. We are moved by the premise that faith is an unseen substance. Faith is the assurance of things unseen. So you see, it leads you to the thing you want, and this is illogical, too. So the whole conversation about spirituality is troublesome to most people, because most people—and I have experienced this—trust in the senses. You know, I trust what I see and touch.

Does faith enable us to deal with the world around us better?

I can only say that if faith is structured in the precepts of one's, let's say, religion in the Judeo-Christian sense. If I could speak this way: Faith lets us deal with the world if faith is guided by Scripture and by the teachings of the spiritual elders and conversations with your spiritual director or rabbi or whomever. It's not just, "I'll just have faith in whatever I feel like." Faith trusts a scaffolding of promises—scriptural promises—that keep you on the straight and narrow. And one is always recollecting, one is always coming back to a faith that *does* help you overcome the world. For example, I've been thinking for many years about the precept of being last—about the line that says who would be first should go last. Well, on the world's face of it, that doesn't make much sense. We're taught to go for the gusto, the biggest first. So one must have faith that the line is true, or one is insane to follow it, right? Without faith, that Biblical precept makes no sense at all. With faith, it is sublime.

You remind me of the Welsh writer Gwyn Thomas who wrote Don't Expect the World to Make Sense. *There is something you wrote in* A Way Without Words, *and I want to quote it here for a moment: "Autonomy, independent thought and action, is critical to the psychological maturity on which spiritual growth depends." Can you explain that? Autonomy meaning "be by yourself" or "be solitary," or how do you mean autonomy?*

Healthy autonomy means to be an independent, integrated person, whose ground of being is healthfully solid. Autonomy is essential to wholeness, because otherwise one can be led around by the nose by any strong, charismatic person who tells you black is white and white is black. One needs to weigh ideas, be able to think for one's self. To figure out answers for one's self. This theme has been running through my work since I began writing. This also reinforces the point about faith: One must be responsible, since there are consequences to living by faith and not by sight, as it says in the Bible. Number one, faith is not popular. Two, it's illogical. Three, it's risky business. With faith, one is vulnerable, on the cutting edge of one's intuitive experience. Four, there's often some suffering because one gives up the supposedly logical material gain that, say, lets other people go first.

To be healthfully autonomous, one has to be a strong, sane, lucid person. That, too, requires independence and objectivity. All of that enters the psychological concept of autonomy. Autonomy doesn't only mean to sit alone on the mountaintop. It does mean to be strong enough to, you know, choose as in the Spanish proverb, "God says, 'Choose what you will and pay for it.'" Healthy, autonomous persons understand this. They pay for their choices. They understand the consequences.

The idea was that somehow you follow what your book title says: Do What You Love, the Money Will Follow. *But you didn't say how much.*

I've had people write me letters and say, "Do what you love, the money will follow, but you didn't say how much or when, and I'm still waiting." I've seen some little cartoons, too, now in the *San Francisco Chronicle*. They've said, "I love Maui, and so the money will follow," and it shows the guy sailing off into the sunset.

What did you mean by that phrase, anyway? Did you really mean that when you do what you love, the money will follow?

I meant that when one invests oneself in one's area of talent, values, competence; and that, moreover, when one does that in a way that one respects—in the incremental minutiae, not the glamour job—the likelihood is that one can earn a living at it. Now there's a certain amount of money per vocation. So that the carpenter makes X amount of dollars, and the city planner or the dynamo Donald Trump or whoever—makes another chunk or another quantity. But enough for one's vocation follows. The only part of that saying—which relates, of course, to vocation— that I'm now dissatisfied with is that I feel that certain nonpaid functions, like parenting, constitute vocation. I've come to see that we must support our vocation like a parent supports a child. For example, I'm a writer and a thinker, not a celebrity. Writers and thinkers, unless they write about sex, money, or presidential wives, are not necessarily rolling in big bucks. One must plan to support a vocation. Here again, coming back to autonomy, one takes the consequences for these vocational choices. But to choose not to practice the vocation is a hell. Because vocation is our innate being longing to express. So who are we to say, "Oh no. I need a new refrigerator, so I cannot honor my God-given talents or my gifts."

There's also the aspect of God that lives in the details.

Yes.

The process of living can actually be a spiritual path?

Oh, definitely.

But particularly so when one identifies one's own deeper calling.

The deeper call may not be a lightning bolt hitting us. It's simply that we each have a way of being in the world. To honor that way of being, to walk in tune with the interior music that we hear, is a great, great gift of life. It *is* life. Anything else is anti-life. This is a miracle, really—if a person is blessed enough to hear that inner music. Many people exist their whole life knowing that there's something happening within that must be expressed. They feel, "I hear it—sort of. I'm not sure what it is." This is why they're tortured: they're not hearing their call clearly. Prayer lets us hear the inner music more clearly.

Joseph Campbell used to talk about hearing the music. He had some wonderful stories that he would tell. He told us this one story about this woman who actually heard music. She was hearing music in her teenage years, and it was like the muse calling. I think somehow if we can open ourselves to that place in us where the music can come through...so often we cover it up because of the pace of our life. We don't slow down enough. We don't have enough silence. We don't have enough solitude. We don't muster the resources to allow the muse to come through to us.

You know, this process is like cultivating soil. You spoke earlier about a little shoot coming up through the concrete. Well, most of us have so concretized our way of being that we're armored. You remember Wilhelm Reich? He wrote of being armored. Whether you see that armor in the musculature or the emotional body or the intellect, when covering up the feelings, the human essence—the dynamic animating essence—cannot come through. This inner silence or meditative walking brings us back full circle to each of us having a spiritual way because each of us is unique. It takes a certain amount of spiritual intelligence to know what to do for ourselves. It's sort of stupid in a way not to know. Yet we are stupefied, and society is now decomposing as we speak because things are getting out of control. Events are happening so fast. Faxes, Fed Exes, and UPS next day, 24 hours and 6-hour. Soon business will want to insert microchips in our teeth. You're going to be receiving data in your dreams. The point is that one has to know when to say no and how to control these technological advantages. They are here for us to use. We are not to be used by them. So when we're on the spiritual walk, we say, "Put everything in its proper place, and just lead a well-ordered, disciplined, quiet, simple life. Take things as they come, but don't get carried away with all the busy-busy techno-jazz."

You've done that in your own life, haven't you?

I have done that in my own life—more and more, really. I trust simplicity. I was reading that Gandhi went off by himself quite frequently. He grew to believe that he could reach more people in silence—through silence—than he could through the media and through his political activities. That's what he did, and that's when he had the biggest impact. This has had a profound meaning for me personally, because I have been living more and more simply, as a contemplative.

Are you referring to his fasts?

No, just the times that he spent alone. Praying, spinning—fasting, also, and brisk, meditative walking—like that. I'm not only proposing that a mindful life—a worshipful life—lets us be calmer, more grounded. To seek the benefits first is to slip into a ditch. Prayer unites us with God, lifts us entirely *out of ourselves* into a sacred union, the outcomes of which are always surprising and cannot be premeditated. We turn within to gain functional power without....

I think of a contemporary teacher named Mother Meera who currently lives in Germany but is from India. She doesn't speak. I mean she speaks, I'm sure, in her regular life, but people just go to be in her presence, to be near her. She doesn't say anything. She doesn't give a lecture. She doesn't give a talk. She doesn't tell people what to do, but people are moved to be with her.

Yes. That's the beauty of worshipful silence. A few years ago, when I cut back on my corporate practice, I began to live just as you describe, just not speaking. Today, you can't reach me by phone, and I now have a little protective set-up that I've grown to trust. I am more productive in this way than in all the previous years. But I've never had any encouragement to do that. I wrote about that in *A Way Without Words*—having cut back travel and so on preceding the writing of that book. You know, in the West, we lack models for simplicity, even lack stories about fictional types who live simply. So all of our monks and mystics tend to be Eastern stories—well, almost all. Everyone said, "No, no—don't live contemplatively—be very careful." It's true, you do have to be prudent, but I've come to trust silence as a marvelous tiller of spiritual soil.

I think of Buckminster Fuller, who took a year out to be silent when he was going through a real personal crisis in his life. He was about the age of 28 or 29, and he took a year of silence. Tara Singh is another spiritual teacher who took a year or two of silence.

Meher Baba, the Indian avatar, lived a silent life all throughout his entire adulthood. I still get mail from his followers because I've quoted him in several works. Meher Baba lived totally in silence from, I guess, the age of 30 until his transition.

There is a spiritual teacher here in Santa Cruz named Baba Hari Das, who is also silent. He has been in this country for several years and uses a blackboard to communicate.

I have many penpals who are monks and nuns in different monasteries. They're living in silence. So of course they liked *Ordinary People as Monks and Mystics.* They loved *A Way Without Words* because it legitimized, in a secular sense, what they have been called to do. Of course they also validated my call by virtue of their way of living. That's how I came to respect silence. I'm not suggesting it's the *only* way of life. This is where I would differ from almost everybody else: I'm proposing we're individuals. There is a fulfilling spiritual life-style for each of us. It takes an enormous amount of courage to live that, to live one's truth.

According to your book Ordinary People as Monks and Mystics, *you actually discovered many people living in the hills of Mendocino County in Northern California who were living their life in this way. You found that the values by which they lived and the manner in which they lived, in many cases, duplicated that of monks and mystics.*

Yes, all over the U.S. and Canada, really. In Pennsylvania there is a strong Quaker tradition, for example, that nurtures such living. The other thing is that I find that the more I look at this pattern of life, the more I find that people who are spiritually intelligent in a broad way are careful about their identifications: They don't squander their attention on just anything. So if you watch TV or movies or read magazines or books or listen to the radio, whatever, there is a way of spending attention that strengthens you and gives life, and there's a way that depletes you. I found many individuals, and I include myself in this, who are careful about what they attend to. That takes us back to your comment about the age we live in and how busy we are. When people say that they are too busy to take time for themselves—that the only time that they have for themselves is when they're driving to work, which is probably one reason that people don't want to give up their car; it's a little protected space, an incubation space where they can go and come in peace—you know, their lives are *too* busy.

Another thing I'm moved to add for those who live with spouses or who have little children is that it takes a long time to teach others how we wish to be treated. Sometimes I get letters from people who say it's a great victory for them when their children realize that, "Oh, this is Mom's time or Dad's quiet time. We don't disturb them now." This is a tremendous breakthrough for an entire family—especially for the adults in the family—when the children learn that lesson. Our friends also must be taught, and it's our responsibility to tell others clearly what we need.

I'd like to give a personal example: Sometimes corporate clients call me on Sunday. Well, I don't speak on the phone on Sunday. I keep what we might call the Sabbath. For a long time, I felt funny about admitting that. (This goes back to our discussion of what the world expects.) Finally, I just told one client who had called me about something—I just sent a message to her fax saying, "I keep Sundays quiet, and I'll call you tomorrow about this." This happens to be a vice president of a thriving firm. She told me later that my fax reminded her of what *she'd* wanted to do for herself for years and years: Namely, keep a day for herself. Sometimes we minimize the importance of our personal disclosures. Yet, they're important for each of us to tell the other.

I know. I have a personal story, too. Dr. Haridas Chaudhuri was the founder of the California Institute of Integral Studies in San Francisco. He used to keep his mornings silent. Up until noon he was unavailable. He would use that time for writing and meditation. Then he would be available from noon to midnight in his work, in his life at the institute, teaching, and so forth. He was very available to people. But that morning time was a very sacred time. So he was not available before noon. Once you knew that, you knew you were just never able to talk to him before noon. But after that, you could reach him. It has always impressed me that this man who was doing so many things was very responsible and had lots of irons in the fire. Yet he made that time for himself.

And more energy. You asked earlier about this spiritual life versus the material benefits. I said that the first thing about this silence is that it lets us be successful. Interior stillness is the way to garner power, true endurance, your staying power, resourcefulness. Independence of thought also comes from inner silence. I'll give you another example: About five or ten years ago, I took January off. I didn't do anything during the month of January. Because I'm in business essentially for myself, I'm able to arrange that. Then two or three years later, I took off during January and February. Then I took January, February, and August. You'd be amazed at the results. My income went up. I was so much more creative. This doesn't make sense, but mysteriously it does. Like your previous example, we tap into living reservoirs of power. The

Bible says our prayer life opens us to living water. A reservoir of living water is gained through whatever disciplined prayer we can muster. Even meditating on one line of Scripture can get us started—that meditation soon becomes a prayer.

Marsha, in the book A Way Without Words—*I guess I would call half of it a manual on how to live, according to some of the things we've been talking about here. One of the things that's in there is the use of sacred texts. You refer to the Psalms, of course, but you also talk about the use of many other sacred texts as well. Why are they important?*

For me, the Psalms and, of course, the Gospels, are embedded with truth about consciousness, the deeper knowledge of God, Christ, and the Holy Spirit. There is embedded, structured, in sacred writing (just as in the traditions that we spoke of earlier) information that is almost secret. Even the cadence of it informs us—structures Truth in our mind. It's like sacred music, too. Certain liturgies and certain requiems—the cadences of these notes and words—draw us deep into meditation. This is why some people fall asleep when they read Scripture. It's like going into church or going to a lecture. Something happens to your mind; it can't quite keep up with the truth. All of a sudden, the sermon is over and you feel fine again. Well, this is because Truth seems like heavy information. It weighs us deep down into ourselves.

Another thing I want to add is that the second half of *A Way Without Words*, Part Two, involves "sessions." I was amazed to find readers trying to rush through those sessions in, say, 45 minutes with a group. You can spend a year on one session. So what stunned me was how quickly people want to read everything, like they consume fast food. My books are not like that. You must take your time to savor ideas. You're not catching a bus. The truths will be there, you know. It's your own little book. I mention that because this is just a part of the malaise of our times—

the fact that we're rushing to gobble up everything. The spiritual life cannot be rushed. My sessions introduce a reflective process. We sit for a minute and recollect ourselves. Maybe listen to a little music. Then read, then we discuss or do journal work. It's very leisurely. Wherever your insight comes, you stop, you notice, and you chew over it a bit.

You let the insight in—you return to it. I don't know if this is relevant. If you read a Bible with a pencil—I happen to underline mine—if I get a new Bible, it's like reading it for the first time. With an old one, my eyes are drawn automatically to the underlinings. This is why I say with some of these books—not only mine, but other, serious writers' books—you should have a couple of copies, and maybe on some anniversary, return to a book that's meant a lot to you and start again. You'll see—you underline different things. You read it afresh. This is certainly how the study of Scripture could be.

What about the use of music? You mention music in the book.

Music isn't bound by our earthly vocabulary. It is a universal language. In fact, I recommend a couple of requiems. There are a couple by Bach—*The Messiah* is one. In some communiqué between Jung and Herman Hesse, I think Hesse writes to Jung that these pieces of music are certain paths to God. This is so. Again, some music is holy—like Scripture. There's celestial information in these languages, and they're nonverbal. They're illogical. They're spiritual. The Christian might say the Holy Spirit is in some music. Maybe the Buddhists would say something else.

EPILOGUE

There is an old Sufi saying to the effect that there are as many spiritual paths as there are souls in the world. Even the Buddha admonished his followers not to do what he said just because he had said it, but rather only if it worked for them in their own lives. Marsha Sinetar reminds us of the truth of both of these spiritual legacies. Each of us is a unique human and spiritual being. We can use the doctrine, teachings, and insights of whatever spiritual tradition, discipline, or practice that calls us, but these are merely guidelines or tools to assist us in the discovery of who we really are, the essential nature of our being. This is beyond all definition or dogma. The true spiritual teacher realizes this and eventually throws his students out, to live their spiritual path on their own. This expulsion is done out of love, not anger. The late J. Krishnamurti said, "Truth is a pathless land," and he often spoke against the idea of following a teacher, and yet he, himself, lectured as a teacher throughout the world during his lifetime. There was this paradox, but even he had previously had teachers, which had led him eventually to abandon them and all other religious trappings.

The point is that we should use all the spiritual wisdom we resonate with and follow whatever we feel is right for us, not because someone tells us so, but because it touches the core of our being. Just as Marsha Sinetar tells us, "Healthy autonomy means to be an independent, integrated person, whose ground of being is healthfully solid."

CHAPTER SIX

MEDITATION:
ESCAPING INTO LIFE

Shinzen Young, with Michael Toms

PROLOGUE

*O*ne *of the most challenging problems we face in life is that we don't know how to concentrate. We live in an era of lethally attractive distractions. Thus, we're easily diverted from our intended goals and lose much of the force of our decisions and insights we might use to guide our lives. We haven't trained ourselves to listen to the quiet, more subtle levels of our mind, body, and emotions. An ability to focus steadily on specific aspects of experience can help immeasurably in enhancing our daily life. Particularly in these times when external events are powerfully compelling, it is useful to be able to hear the inner message of our body/mind.*

Shinzen Young, a native of Los Angeles, became fascinated with Asian culture at an early age, learning Chinese and Japanese while still in his teens. In the late sixties, he entered a doctoral program in Buddhist studies at the University of Wisconsin. Three years later, he was ordained as a Buddhist monk at Mount Koya, Japan. After several years of training in Asian monasteries, he became interested in the scientific study of meditative states and worked at the Princeton Biofeedback Institute. He taught Asian philosophy at Chapman College and mathematics and physics at Ernest Holmes College, and frequently serves as translator for Joshu Sasaki Roshi at Mount Baldy Zen Center. He conducts vipassana (mindfulness meditation) retreats throughout North America. His goal is to make meditative practice a viable path for Westerners, not just an exotic import from the East.

MICHAEL TOMS: *How did you become interested in Buddhism in the first place? How did that happen for you?*

SHINZEN YOUNG: Actually, my initial interest was in the languages of Asia. I was about 14 years old when I saw a samurai movie, and I decided to go to Japanese school even though I'm not of Japanese ancestry. In Los Angeles, we have ethnic language schools that meet after public school. My parents supported me in that. I went every day to Japanese school, so I grew up bilingual and bicultural without ever leaving Los Angeles. That led to my being an exchange student in Japan. I took my senior year there. While I was there, I was mostly interested in language and culture, but I did encounter some people who were practicing Buddhist meditation. I noticed that they seemed very happy, very fulfilled. It's as though they had a secret that they would be willing to share, but they knew they could not force it on you in any way. I sensed a hand extended that I could take if I wished.

When I returned to the United States, I decided to enter a graduate program in Buddhist studies. That was at the University of Wisconsin in the late sixties. It was a glorious time for people interested in things such as Buddhism and Hinduism, and the Wisconsin program was the biggest of its kind in the United States. After completing my Ph.D. coursework, I was sent back to Japan to research my thesis, which was to be on the Shingon School of Buddhism. Shingon is a form of Vajrayana related to the Tibetan practices, but preserved in Japan. When I got there, I found that they wouldn't let me study it intellectually. I had to actually practice it. So I stayed as a meditating monk for a number of years at Mount Koya.

Isn't it interesting that a Vajrayana school from Tibet would make its way into Japan. How did that happen?

Well, the answer to that question is interesting, but it requires a little historical background. At the risk of oversimplification, I would say that there are three main streams of Buddhist practice: Vipassana, Zen, and Vajrayana. Each is traditionally associated with one of three distinct cultural regions in Asia, although they all ultimately go back to developments in India.

The history of Buddhism on its native soil of India spans some 17 centuries, from the time of the Buddha who lived in the 6th century B.C., until the end of the 12th century A.D., when Moslem hordes finally overran the heartland of Buddhism in northeast India. These 17 centuries can be roughly divided into 3 periods, early (first 5 centuries), middle (next 7 centuries) and late (last 5 centuries). The early period preserved a practice style fairly close to that of the Buddha himself. This is known historically as Hinayana, or Small Vehicle. The middle period saw the rise of the Mahayana, or Great Vehicle; and finally, Vajrayana, or the Diamond Vehicle, developed during the late period.

Hinayana is today preserved as the Theravada School, centered primarily in Southeast Asia, especially Sri Lanka, Burma, and Thailand. Its representative practice is vipassana (mindfulness meditation). In vipassana, high concentration is used to meticulously examine the fine structure of one's subjective world. This leads to "insight," a radically new understanding about the nature of self and experience. One might compare this process to the work of a scientist who discovers a new paradigm through investigating the fine structure of the objective world using an awareness of an extending tool, such as a microscope. Mindfulness is the microscope of the mystic.

Mahayana Buddhism reached China from India through the Central Asian trade routes. There, over a period of many centuries, it became highly modified under the influence of Chinese culture. The best-known school of Chinese Buddhism is Chan. Chan spread from China into the other countries of East Asia: Korea, Japan, and Vietnam. In the West, Chan is usually known by its Japanese name, Zen. Actually, there are two main schools of Zen in Japan, and they are quite different in outlook: Soto Zen practices "just sitting," while Rinzai Zen encourages solving koans such as: "How do you manifest the sound of one hand clapping?" Since a koan cannot be solved through thinking, it creates great confusion in the mind of the meditator. Eventually, one learns to abide continuously in this confusion without needing to do anything about it. Thus, the drivenness to understand is gradually worked through. The mind then thinks without needing to think. This mode of thinking leads to intuitive insight.

Vajrayana is preserved mainly in the Tibetan and Himalayan cultural region. The practice of Vajrayana centers around elaborate rituals, which are actually sequences of meditation techniques. One important aspect of these rituals involves replacing your usual self-image with that of a vividly visualized spiritual archetype. This engenders insight into the arbitrary nature of the self-identification process.

So now you have the broad outline of Asian Buddhism. Three vehicles developing in India during three periods, now associated with three cultural regions of Asia, and practicing three distinct methods for reaching similar enlightenment.

But as I mentioned, this is something of an oversimplification. For one thing, a trickle of Indian Vajrayana reached China during the Tang Dynasty. From China it was brought to Japan in the early ninth century. Then it died out in China, but it has remained an important school in Japan, where it is called the Shingon or Mantra School. So, Japanese Vajrayana is related to that of Tibet, in the sense that they share a common ancestor going back to late Indian Buddhism.

Interesting. What was life like in the monastery? Can you give us a little insight into that?

If I had to characterize it in a single word, I would say that it was transformative. I suppose that a lot of people think of a monastery as a place you go to get away from things, a kind of escapism. But, a monastery is a giant feedback device, a place where you can learn.

The general tenor of life there is that you don't get much sleep; you do physical labor and you have formal periods of sitting meditation practice. The physical tasks are simple, so you can practice maintaining a meditative state while you do them. Doing the same no-brainer work for hours every day is either hellishly boring or celestially delightful, depending on whether you know how to enter the "flow state" of high concentration while you do it.

You would rise at, what, 3:00 A.M.?

Yes, something like that. At the time I had difficulty understanding the sleep-deprivation aspect. I had always heard that

Buddhist practice was supposed to be the middle way between self-indulgence and self-torture. Managing on four hours of sleep seemed somewhat skewed to the torture side. But later, I came to understand the lesson that they were trying to teach us. There is a difference between objective fatigue and subjective fatigue. Subjective fatigue is the yucky feeling you get when you are tired. Objective fatigue is the actual physical state of your body. What happens is that as soon as a person starts to feel tired or sleepy, it produces uncomfortable body sensations. We tend to resist and congeal around such sensations. This produces a kind of inner friction that wastes energy. Whenever you resist any feeling, you are fighting with yourself. It's equivalent to an engine grinding against itself. So you use up a lot of energy in fighting with the way that the tiredness makes you feel subjectively. That makes you more tired objectively. By being forced to go with little sleep, you learn how not to fight with the yucky, subjective feelings that come when you get tired. This frees up a lot of objective energy, which you can use to live your life. You discover that you don't need as much rest as you think.

People frequently claim that they're too busy to take time out of their day for meditation. I ask them, "How many hours do you sleep each night?" Usually it's about eight. Regular practice of meditation changes one's physiology. Experienced meditators can get by easily with five or six hours sleep. If people take an hour out of each day to meditate, they actually experience a net gain of an hour or so in extra time available for life.

It seems like you must have taken to this as a duck to water. Is that true?

Not really. It was a big struggle at the beginning. I would say it was actually sort of hell for the first couple of years. I am an academician by training. Thinking is my great joy. Initially when I tried to meditate, my mind would constantly wander into fantasies, judgment, planning, and intellectual speculation. My body was fidgety, my legs ached, and I struggled with sleepiness. Probably the only reason I kept doing it was that I was stuck there in Japan and had committed myself to it. I don't think I would have stayed with it if I hadn't set up the situation so I couldn't get out of it. I used to wonder, "What am I doing in this samurai boot camp?" But eventually my mind did quiet down, and I began to experience what is called samadhi or one-pointedness—first only during sitting, and then also in the midst of daily life. Later, I learned that a similar state is known and cultivated in all the spiritual traditions of the world. In Christianity it is called the "prayer of quiet." Samadhi is the most powerful and universal skill that any human being can acquire. All other human endeavors from the mundane to the spiritual become dramatically catalyzed when pursued in a state of samadhi.

I think the image, particularly in the United States, that many Americans have of monastic life—especially in Japan or Asia— is that it is quite rigorous. It's very challenging to adopt such a lifestyle in the beginning.

Yes, it is rigorous, but fortunately it's also unnecessary! Nowadays, you can find short, user-friendly retreats just about everywhere in North America. My personal mission in life is to figure out new ways of doing the practice, which are suited to this culture, so that people can get really significant experiences without going to "Buddhist boot camp." So far, the results have been encouraging.

So you came back from Japan to the United States, and you decided not to live in Japan any longer. Was there a particular reason for that? Or did you just want to come back home?

The whole point of monastic training is not to learn to be comfortable in a monastery, but to learn to be comfortable anywhere. My first teacher kept a picture by his desk. It was entitled "Buddha Leaving the Mountain." It was an important icon for him. He emphasized to me that the ultimate expression of what I was learning in the monastery would be to return to ordinary life and interact with people in service. I had spent the first half of my life trying to become as Asian as possible. The technology of internal exploration known as meditation represents the pinnacle of Asian culture, its crowning achievement and greatest contribution to the culture of the world. Having encountered that pinnacle, I no longer needed to do the Asia trip. I wanted to come back home and spend the second half of my life making meditation as Western as possible.

If you were to tell us a story that would best capture the essentials of your teacher, what would that story be?

Just before I was to be ordained as a monk, the abbot approached me with a piece of paper. "This is the *homyo* (dharma name) I am considering for you. Do you think it's okay?" he asked. On the paper, starkly calligraphed, were two Chinese characters pronounced Shinzen in Japanese. *Shin* means truth, and *zen* (which is not the same character as in Zen Buddhism), means goodness. I was stunned, because I immediately grasped the significance of the two characters. They stood for the two essential elements that comprised any really mature spiritual path. I stammered something like: "It's beautiful, but I doubt I can live up to it." He continued: "That may be, but are you okay with it as your name?" I said, "Sure." So he gave me a name that would always remind me of the basics. That was 30 years ago.

In the Buddhist tradition, the word *truth* implies insight, clear experiential knowledge of the effortless impersonal process that underlies all our experiences. Through insight, one learns to consciously participate in that process. When you do so, to a certain extent, you transcend the human condition, go beyond your limited personal identity. But this alone does not constitute a complete spiritual path. Goodness is also needed. Goodness implies the ability to manifest a personal self engaged with one's fellow beings. Goodness finds its ultimate expression in a life of effortless service. To transcend the human condition, to improve the human condition, and to understand the complementary relationship between these two—this is the essence, this is our basic job. Liberating insight without service is spiritually narrow. On the other hand, attempting to help people without at least some tools of transcendence leaves one susceptible to burnout and distortions in behavior.

But I am afraid all this may sound somewhat abstract. Let me try to make it more tangible.

Like a precious diamond, liberating insight has many facets. One of these facets is knowing how to pass through the unavoidable physical and emotional pain of life, really feel it, and yet not suffer because of it. The concept of pain without suffering may seem like an oxymoron. Does it hurt? Yes! Does that eclipse the perfection of the moment? No! In fact, it *is* the perfection of the moment.

It is of the utmost importance to understand the difference between pain and suffering. When you understand this, your sense of security is no longer dependent on the vagaries of circumstance. Furthermore, when you understand the difference between pain and suffering, you understand the difference between being motivated by feelings and being driven by them. And you understand how to be deeply empathetic without getting your energy drained.

Suffering is a function of two variables: pain itself and the resistance to the pain. By resistance, I mean interference with the natural flow pattern of the pain. Unfortunately, resistance starts deep within the pre-conscious processing of the nervous system.

Thus, by the time we are consciously aware of a wave of pain, it has already been congealed into a mass of suffering. That is why pain is equated with suffering by most people.

But suffering equals pain multiplied by resistance (roughly speaking). This is true whether the pain is physical, or something emotional like anger, sadness, fear, embarrassment, or remorse. If you consistently apply this insight to various types of pain, the habit of resistance gets trained away at progressively deeper levels of neural processing. Eventually, you are able to have the literally earth-shaking experience of pure pain. Pure pain is pain unmixed with resistance. Pure pain causes little suffering, no matter how intense it may be. Moreover, pure pain purifies. Its energy kneads the substance of your soul, working out the kinks and lumps for you.

Pure pain purifies, but suffering makes a person brittle and dehumanized. Those who follow the path of self-mortification need to be very clear about this point.

Of course, everything that I have said about pain is also true of pleasure in a converse sort of way. Suffering is directly proportional to how much we resist against the pain. Satisfaction is *inversely* proportional to how much we grasp on to the pleasure. The less we grasp the flow of pleasure, the greater the satisfaction derived from it. And of course, pure pleasure purifies.

So, one facet of insight relates to learning how to experience pleasure and pain in a radically new way. But how is this actually done? Well, you develop focus power through meditation practice. This allows you, upon occasion, to so fully affirm the moment-by-moment reality of an experience that you have no time left to congeal that experience into a rigid object, and no space left to maintain a sense of self, separate from the experience. You and the experience disappear into completeness. It's everything and nothing at the same time: "*Todo y nada,*" as St. John of the Cross put it.

So, one facet of liberating insight involves learning how to diminish suffering and elevate satisfaction through having complete experiences of pleasure and pain. Another facet involves the ability to have a complete experience of yourself, the feeling/thinking ego, your limited identity. When you have a complete experience of feeling/thinking self, you become free from it. You so fully affirm the moment-by-moment experience of self-consciousness that you have no time left to congeal that self-consciousness into an object extended in time and space. Everything that is contractive in yourself collapses inward toward a dimensionless point. Everything that is expansive in yourself dissipates outward toward infinity. You embrace all of creation from within and without. The two fundamental forces of nature (expansion and contraction) separate, tearing apart the very fabric of the self. The self dissolves back into those forces and becomes them. Then, because there is no solidified self lodged between them, the forces of expansion and contraction can directly touch each other. They commingle and cancel each other out. There are then no force waves to stir time, space, self, or world into existence. There is only true peace, the peace that passeth understanding.

By having such experiences many, many times, one learns to perceive all of creation as not fundamentally separate from one's self. Love, compassion, and the desire to serve arise spontaneously. So this brings us to service, goodness, the second essential of the spiritual path. Just as insight has many facets, so also with service. I would like to talk about just one aspect, an aspect that the Dalai Lama emphasizes a lot—compassion.

Compassion is practiced in two ways: subtly and overtly. You can subtly serve any person with whom you interact by allowing their poison and pain to resonate deeply within you, and experiencing it completely so that it does not turn into suffering within you. This is the healthy alternative to both callous indifference and enervating enmeshment.

This subtle service is a natural extension of the self-liberation process. You purified your own pain by willingly experiencing it with mindfulness and equanimity. Now, in daily interaction, you open yourself up to other people's pain. But you apply mindfulness and equanimity to it as it resonates within you. By experiencing another person's pain in this liberated way, you are subtly, subliminally helping them to do the same. People want to have you around, but they cannot say exactly why. The reason is that your body is constantly preaching a wordless sermon to everybody you interact with, even casually. It's deeply fulfilling to share (com) the pain (passion), but *not* share the suffering.

Subtle is significant, but we must also serve in a more overt, tangible way. The form that this overt service takes depends on our personal interests and abilities and on the norms of the culture in which we live. For some, it's expressed in how they raise their families. For others, it will take the form of social action or helping professions. Some may express it through the use of special powers, such as the ability to heal. For many, overt service takes the form of teaching and supporting people's spiritual practice.

So, my teacher conveyed the entire richness of the path in the two characters he chose to name me with.

You mentioned suffering. As you were describing the qualities of your teacher and what he taught you, it reminded me of that Thomas Merton quote—about how he entered the monastery to practice suffering more effectively.

Yes, I use that quote all the time in my retreats. I don't remember it exactly, either, but I think it was something like: "I didn't become a monk to suffer more than other people. I became a monk to suffer more effectively." People often don't understand what he meant by that. It's actually quite a profound statement. What it means is that physical or psychological discomfort in and of itself does not have to turn into suffering. There's another factor. I call that factor the degree of one's skill at feeling. It's an interesting concept. That feeling is a skill. This skill can either be developed or not. Most people do not have it very highly developed, unfortunately. That leads to big problems like injustice, exploitation, abuse, war, and genocide. People wonder why these things happen. I believe they happen because we don't take time to cultivate skills at feeling. Skill at feeling means, well, let me give a tangible example. What kind of feeling would you like me to talk about? It's the same for every kind of feeling.

Anger.

Let's say you turn on the television and you see something that angers you. You say, "I'm really angry." We can perceive that experience of anger more precisely. What do we really mean when we say "I'm angry"? As you know, I'm interested in mathematics and science. One of the things mathematicians are always trying to do is called analysis or decomposition. They try to take a complex process and break it down into its components so that they can get a handle on it. Well, one way to analyze the experience of anger (or any negative emotion, for that matter) is to see that it consists of two components. If we can keep track of these two components, we can handle our emotions much better. One component is a sequence of thought in your mind—internal conversations and internal images. The other component is a sequence of feelings in your body-body sensations. What we call an emotion is a tangling together of thought and feeling. If we can untangle these components *as the emotion is happening*, keep track of them, know what part is thought and what part is feeling, we discover that the emotion causes much less suffering. Suffering drives and distorts one's behavior, creating big problems in the objective world. In other words, if you can bring enough mindfulness and acceptance to a negative emotion as it is happening, it ceases to cause suffering. Yet, where has it gone? You haven't run away from it. You've merely experienced it with extraordinary clarity. You've escaped *into* it.

So we haven't run away from it; we've escaped into it.

Exactly! If I were required to give a "quick and dirty" definition of meditation, it would be that meditation is the practice of
escaping into life. It's escape in the sense that one does not feel
limited by the mind/body process or the surrounding situation.
But, the direction of escape is not from what's happening, but
rather into it.

This is very challenging. It's challenging to understand, and
it's challenging to do. The experience of escaping into something
is totally different from merely being passionately involved in it.
When we ingenuously try to describe this experience, it comes
out sounding like we are playing with words, fabricating para-
doxes to shock or impress people. Escaping into something simply means having a radically complete experience of it. A radically complete experience is rich and fulfilling, but it is also
empty and transparent. I sometimes say that we Buddhists are our
own worst public relations representatives because our vocabulary seems designed to turn people off. You know, we are always
talking about emptiness, no self, void.

Nothingness.

Yes, but the nothingness of the mystic is a very special kind
of nothingness. The *nihil* of Meister Eckhart is not the nihil of
nihilism. The *nada* of St. John of the Cross is not "nada."
Nothingness is a *terminus technicus*, a well-defined technical
term in the vocabulary of world mysticism.

Hinduism, Buddhism, Judaism, Christianity, Islam, and
Taoism differ radically in their beliefs and customs. Yet, the mys-
tics who represent the core of these traditions often speak of the
Spiritual Source as a special kind of nothing. Historically, this
can only partially be explained as the result of mutual influences.
Despite what some New Age books would have you believe,

these formulations arose independently in India, China, and the West before there was significant contact. So, we are faced with some fascinating questions. Why should they agree on such a counter-intuitive (if not downright offensive) description of God when they disagree in so many other areas? And furthermore, why does the mystic's description of the awesome creative power of nothingness sound so similar to contemporary theories of cosmology and quantum physics? Is it coincidence or convergence?

As a person of Jewish ancestry, I find it deeply satisfying that the description of God's creative activity as it appears in the Kabbalah is remarkably parallel to that of my teacher Joshu Sasaki Roshi, contemporary Japanese Zen Master. The goal of Jewish meditation is to experience *Briah yesh me ayn*. In Hebrew: *Briah* (the creation) *yesh* (of things) *me* (from) *ayn* (nothing). *Ayn* is synonymous with *Ha Makom*, the Source, i.e., God. Moreover, in Kabbalah, creation is conceived as happening continuously. God literally loves us into existence each moment through the oscillating interplay of *hesed* (expansion) and *gevurah* (contraction).

Physicists speak of the creative power of quantum fluctuations of the void. This *seems* remarkably similar to the descriptions of mystics, especially Buddhist mystics. At the very least, it provides us with some wonderful metaphors. The enlightened people of the world can now stand up and say, "I know that what I'm trying to describe to you sounds weird and paradoxical, but it's not any weirder than these widely accepted theories of science, and as a matter of fact, it's rather similar to them."

Like not being able to tell the difference between the particle and the wave.

Yes, the concept of wave-particle complementarity is extremely useful in explaining certain aspects of meditative experience. The basic idea behind complementarity is that objects can be looked upon either as waves or particles. "Particle" does not necessarily imply "small." Any chunk of matter is a particle—a bowling ball, or the earth itself. Associated with every particle is its wave function.

When you think about it, it's absolutely astonishing, because particles and waves seem to be so fundamentally different. Particles are rigid and separate—two billiard balls recoil if they collide. Waves are bending and interactive—two water waves immediately merge upon contact. Particles have established boundaries and fixed centers. Waves expand and contract. A particle retains scratches and is vulnerable to shattering force. If you attempt to scratch or shatter a wave, it simply digests the energy of the attack into itself.

The practical implication of complementarity lies in the fact that some applications work better from the wave perspective, while other applications work better from the particle perspective. The issue boils down to knowing which perspective is appropriate, and the fact that the engineer always has the freedom to choose either one.

Spiritual freedom is very much like this. For some life applications, we must congeal the mind and body into a separate particular person—for example, when you need to figure stuff out or negotiate a contract. The problem is that most people are *limited* to the particulate perspective only. They are unable to immediately switch to the undulatory paradigm when they encounter situations that work better with the wave self. What situations are those? Well, let me give you just a few representative examples: enjoying a morsel of food, experiencing bereavement, making love, being embarrassed in public, and praying.

Once again, the issue here is freedom—freedom to adopt the most appropriate perspective. If you cannot dissolve into a wave, you are missing out on a lot of life. Naturally, death is frightening. Indeed, there are human experiences for which the wave self is not only appropriate, but absolutely essential. To attempt to pass through these experiences while maintaining a separate particulate self causes unspeakable suffering. Acute physical or emotional pain, chronic pain, and, of course, death itself, are in this category.

I'd like to focus for a moment on thoughts, because I think there's a key here. I recall Krishnamurti talking about thoughts being from the past. They're always from the past. They're never from the present. There's this idea in Buddhism that thoughts are just another sense gate, like hearing, seeing, smelling, tasting, and body sensation.

Yes, absolutely, a sense mode.

But there's this other image that thoughts are bad. That somehow we have to go beyond the thoughts. What about that dichotomy? On the one hand, thoughts are just another sense, and on the other hand, thoughts are the enemy of meditation.

The problem is not thinking, per se, but the fact that thinking is subject to so much drivenness, fixation, and lack of clarity. In fact, spiritual wisdom is just ordinary thought, functioning without being driven by the need for answers!

The Buddhist tradition analyzes the meditation process into two aspects: calming and clarifying. But there is no real clear-cut distinction between these two; it is more a matter of emphasis. If you emphasize the calming aspect of meditation, then you may try to pull away from thought, weaken its grasp, cool it out. There are numerous strategies for achieving this. For example, you can count your breaths or focus on a mantra or visualize a small disc of light, etc.

If you emphasize the clarifying aspect of meditation, then you might actually take thought itself as your object of meditation. This means that you analyze thought into its components as they arise and observe these components with a hands-off attitude. In this case, you have no particular agenda to control or quiet the thinking process.

Thought arises through internal speech (verbal thinking) and internal images (visual thinking). In each instant, your conscious thinking process must involve one or both of these components. At this moment, is your thinking process visual, verbal, or both? If visual, look *through* the images, not *at* them. If the images persist, fine, continue to look through them and be aware; does the rate of transition from image to image remain constant or speed up or slow down? If the image dies away as soon as you notice it, fine, but be clear; is the internal screen then completely blank or is there some "snow" or subtle stirring on it? If it's the former, enjoy the peacefulness of the blank screen. Abide there, ready to detect the first buds of the next visual thought. If it's the latter, carefully watch those remnant movement qualities. Give them permission to speed up or slow down. You are now literally observing the energy envelope of your unconscious mind as it processes!

If the thought arises as internal conversation, fine, listen to the words as just so many sounds, like listening to birds chirping. Be clear: Is it your voice or someone else's voice that's talking in your head? Is the speech coming in complete sentences, short phrases, or individual words? Is the loudness and speed of that internal voice constant, or does it fluctuate? If the internal words die away as soon as you notice them, fine. If they persist, that's fine, too; just listen with detachment. When the words die away, are your "internal loud speakers" completely silent, or is there some remnant "tape hiss"? If there is no activity whatsoever in your internal loudspeakers, then continuously listen to the peacefulness and enjoy it. If there is some subtle remnant of activity, let it flow. It represents subconscious verbal processing.

By working with thought in this way, eventually you'll come to the literally earth-shaking experience of complete thinking. Thought ceases to be a thing and breaks up into an energy wave.

You become so fascinated with the moment-by-moment movement qualities of thought that you are no longer caught up in its meanings. Put another way, every thought that is experienced completely has the same meaning. The meaning is release and purification of consciousness!

So, this is the process of clarifying thought. Thought first becomes clear in the sense that its components can be discriminated distinctly. At the culmination of this discrimination process, thinking becomes so clear that it literally becomes transparent and is no longer in the way.

Earlier you mentioned a song and how it relates to what you've been talking about relative to the meditative state.

Yes, this is a song my friend Shelly Young wrote, based on her experiences in meditation. It is entitled "Aniccha."

Aniccha means impermanence in Pali, the language of the early Buddhist texts. Remember how I said that we Buddhists tend to use "negative vocabulary"? In early Buddhism, the concept of *aniccha* was closely linked to the concept of *dukkha*, the suffering nature of existence. Everything is constantly changing, passing. Even when we seem to experience comfort and stability, we are constantly being goaded by subtle change at a microscopic level. And at the macroscopic level, we live under a sword of Damocles because everything that we depend on for fulfillment will pass—perhaps sooner, perhaps later.

All this is certainly true, but there is much, much more to impermanence than this pessimistic philosophy! As our meditation experiences grow, we begin to become intimate with the flow patterns of impermanence: how it expands, contracts, circulates, and vibrates through all six senses and at all scales of time and space. Once you can detect the natural flow of your senses, you can learn to yield to that flow. Then suffering goes away and is replaced by the joy of purification, the joy of complete experience, and the joy of participating in God's creative process. Impermanence becomes an ally.

At first, you meditate *on* impermanence, but eventually you are meditated *by* impermanence. The flow of impermanence massages the substance of your soul. This aspect of impermanence relates to what in Western religion is called acquiring the Holy Spirit, and to what in Chinese medicine is called activating *qi* (ch'i). It is a kind of inner peristalsis that breaks up and digests experience, absorbing what is nutritive, and excreting what is toxic. You can literally feel the poison and pain within you being churned to the surface and evaporating away. This is called "the joy of purification."

I have tried to describe to you how, when you experience anything completely, it presents its wave nature. It becomes *aniccha*. You stay with that wave, instant by instant, as it dies away into the abundant nothingness of God. All the richness of the experience has been digested into the wave, and all the energy of the wave gets stored in the nothingness. Thus, impermanence marks the path to completeness and to the true peace of God. Other paths to nothingness may lead to nihilism, confusion, and despair. It's interesting how in Hebrew, peace (*shalom*) and completeness (*shalem*) are closely related.

Impermanence also marks the path from nothingness back to somethingness. Inevitably, nothingness, zero, repolarizes into plus and minus, expansion and contraction. You experience yourself and your surrounding scene being gestated into existence within the vibrating folds of God's formless womb. Once again, you have an individual particulate self. But you understand it in a radically new way! You know for sure whence you come, whither you will return, and within what you always abide.

Shinzen, our readers may want to move in the direction you're suggesting. What might be a first step?

I would say that the most important thing is to find a support structure for your practice and a group with which you can do regular sitting retreats. Don't be too concerned with searching for the perfect cosmic guru. But you will probably need a coach, someone with deep meditation experience who also has good communication skills. Spiritual bookstores are good places to go for information networking. See what is available in your area and which approach to meditation appeals to you. Two very useful information resources from my tradition are *Buddhist America,* by Don Morrealle, and *The Inquiring Mind*, a vipassana newsletter published in Berkeley, California. If you would like some personal help in getting set up in a practice, feel free to talk to the staff at my organization, the Vipassana Support Institute, in Los Angeles, California.

If you would like information on Shinzen's programs, a catalog of his tapes, or help getting set up in a mindfulness meditation practice, write or call the Vipassana Support Institute (VSI), 4070 Albright Ave., Los Angeles, CA 90066, (310) 915-1943.

EPILOGUE

The tools and insights Shinzen Young provides have come from a lineage and meditation technology developed over many centuries of contemplative exploration. These are techniques within a framework intended to help one practice meditation. You're not required to adopt a doctrine in order to apply the methods suggested by Shinzen Young. This is the fundamental simplicity of the contemplative way. Anyone can do it. All that is needed is a commitment. As Shinzen suggests, any time given to meditation practice should result in extra time and energy available for other activities.

As the pace of life quickens and the demands on our time increase, it is even more important that we set a priority of being with ourselves for some quiet moments alone. Make it doable. Don't overload yourself. If you can't put aside an hour, do a half hour or 15 minutes. What's most important is to allocate the time, make the commitment, and do it.

Meditation, whatever form it may take, is the doorway to living a more fulfilling and joyful life. It is the path to self-discovery and a limitless panorama of sacred possibilities.

CHAPTER SEVEN

THE POWER OF HEALING IMAGERY

Jeanne Achterberg, with Michael Toms

PROLOGUE

M *ost of us know that we can worry ourselves sick, because we've done it. But few of us are equally aware that we can image ourselves well. We miss the reality that positive visions can have on our health and well-being. Contrary to the modern separation of mind and body, mostly observed in medicine today, how we think—in other words, our mind—can literally transform disease and maintain optimum health. The facts are that this approach to healing has been with us far longer than technological medicine. Yet up until recently, it has been relegated to the realm of quackery. However, the light is returning, as a number of pioneers are leading the way to the rediscovery of the impor-*

tant role that the mind can play in the healing process.

One of these health-care visionaries is Jeanne Achterberg. She has specialized in the application of imaging to physical disease and trauma through work with catastrophic disease and serious illness, and she has received international recognition for her pioneering research in medicine and psychology. A faculty member for 11 years at Southwestern Medical School, University of Texas, Jeanne is currently a professor of psychology at Saybrook Institute in San Francisco. She also has co-chaired the Mind/Body Interventions ad hoc panel for the Office of Alternative Medicine, National Institutes of Health. Her books include Imagery and Healing: Shamanism and Modern Medicine; Woman as Healer; *and her newly published book,* Rituals of Healing.

MICHAEL TOMS: *Jeanne, my first question is: When did you start becoming enamored of imaging and imagery as a way to heal?*

JEANNE ACHTERBERG: That's an interesting question, and I've often thought, How did I get into this business? It occurred to me that I've always been interested in this area. When I grew up, we were itinerant in many ways. My father was in the Service, and books were my friends, as they were for so many children who were by themselves a lot. I used to clear out the shelves on two topics: miracles and witchcraft, much to the dismay of the librarian and my mother. It has occurred to me again in recent years that they're really about the same thing. They're about magic. They're about the possibilities of the human mind. There are hints of a mystery there that we really don't understand. I pursued that as a hobby. Tried to get into Duke at the time that there was a program in parapsychology. I didn't have enough math, and said, "The heck with it," and went on into physiology, which has stood me in good stead. I focused most of my work on brain-behavior relationships, again leading somewhat of a charmed life. I found out there was a young physician named Carl Simonton working in Fort Worth. I was teaching psychology at the time and invited him to talk to my classes. I offered my services as a researcher for a year and pretty much developed a similar philosophical bias.

Tell us about the Simontons' work with the relationship between the mind and body.

Carl and Stephanie Simonton developed the ideas that cancer could be treated not only with modern medicine but with certain mental procedures. It was absolutely necessary to begin a re-examination of one's life. Part of the controversy surrounding their work, of course, involves the notion that we may create consciously or unconsciously our disease processes. Therefore, we can also uncreate them by changing our behaviors, changing our thoughts, and changing our lifestyle.

Imaging has been with us for a long time—eons, millennia. You immediately make the connection between the shamanic path, imaging, and healing. I thought it was interesting that you did that. Perhaps you can tell us why you did that.

I've been interested in imagery, whatever that means to people. To me it does not mean just visualization. It's a very complex, personalized thing that includes all the senses. But I wanted to go to experts. I wanted to go to people who seemed intuitively to be practicing healing with the imagination, and I was led very naturally to the shamans. There are few in existence. There's some anthropological lore that was valuable to study.

Can you give us an example of a shaman?

Michael Harner, who is an anthropologist, speaks the language of science, but he also studied with the Jivaro and is very knowledgeable about the North American Indian tribes and teaches the old ways. It's very important that somebody be willing to understand them and go out and teach. We did a little bit of work with a Huichol tradition, also, and a lot of reading. The shamans, whether we like it or not, have treated the majority of serious illness on this planet from the beginning, and they continue to do so. When nothing else works, we go to people who are practicing shamanlike techniques. My question was: What are they, number one. And number two: Do they work? It's very important. Is this just a rumor that we've perpetrated through our own desire to believe that there's something that can be done with the human mind? Or that someone else's mind can affect my body?

What did you find?

If it is a rumor, it is a persistent one. The problem that I have, and anybody that was raised in the tradition of American medicine will have, is that in the shamanic systems there is a different definition of healing. It has very little to do with healing the tissues of the body. They have a different definition of health. If we accept their definition, which may include things like spiritual health, harmony, and balance, then yes, their healing techniques work. If we are looking exclusively for tissue change, then they also probably work. The problem is that no credible scientist has been willing to go and study these phenomena, and even if they did, they may be hard pressed at this point in time to find any pocket of activity.

In some respects, in the present way science is conducted, it's difficult to research these kinds of practices in that framework.

Absolutely. There is no paradigm for studying how well three days of shamanic work affects individuals, or how well that helps them integrate back into the community. We simply don't understand those things well enough.

However, one of the chapters that got left out of your book is about quantum physics, which does present a scientific paradigm for understanding the shamans' work.

Yes, it does. Quantum physics (just like biochemistry or any other level of science) is only analogy, but it's an acceptable analogy to the scientific mind—one that has led us out of much of our skepticism about this work.

It seems that there is a surface reason as well as a deeper reason for disregarding anything that doesn't have to do with logic and the rational way of looking at things. Why do you think we so often disregard these methods as quackery, or as something not worth pursuing?

I think it's a real issue of protection, of one's belief system, education, and the existing paradigm. It's absolutely necessary in the mind, consciously or unconsciously, for most scientists to protect what they know.

So it's a defensive reaction.

It's a defensive reaction. If what we're saying is true, it would, in the first instance, make the current practice of medicine be considered malpractice. There would be no way that a physician would be allowed to treat a cancer patient or a person who had a heart attack without also dealing with their spiritual needs, their psychological needs, and their community needs. They simply could not, if what we are saying is true. This would create chaos in a medical system that is already in a major crisis. Therefore, I understand those reasons. It's to sustain a stability in a system that has worked very well in many ways.

The truth is that we don't know what gets people well. I have incredible patients that come to me with all sorts of disorders and diseases that either can't be treated or can't be diagnosed by modern medicine. My advice is always to try everything. It took a lot of things to get you sick. Now it's going to take a lot of things to get you well, but especially, it's going to take the thing that you believe in. If you don't know what to believe in, then you need to begin a journey. Find out what it is. In truth, many of them only believe in allopathic medicine, and if that's the case, then that's where they need to go. The rest of it is a waste of time.

You had some interesting references in your book Imagery and Healing, *actually stories of accounts of doctors and the way they said things to patients. The doctor's attitude and its relationship to how the patient felt or became well or sicker. It occurs to me that I think so often that's missed, too. I was thinking about how we choose doctors. We should look for a doctor who can make us feel better when we go to them rather than making us feel worse. I guess we need to pay attention to that.*

Exactly. There's such power that they have. Every nod of their head when they touch a patient's shoulder means more than they could ever imagine in terms of the healing process. We, in truth, have cloaked them in the myth of the shaman. What they do has nothing to do with shamanism, but they serve in that role in our culture.

They're authority figures.

They're authority figures, and authority figures have the power to heal. There's no question about it. Or at least the power to allow people to heal themselves.

So I wonder how many medical schools have courses or classes in the fact that you're about to assume the mantle of an authority figure. How do you assume that mantle with integrity and ethics?

An interesting thing was about to happen in medicine in 1982, which you may be familiar with. There was a blue-ribbon committee appointed to decide how the direction of medical education should go. The document that came out was probably the most important document since the Flexner Report in 1910, which totally redirected medicine toward the allopathic scientific mode and away from the homeopathic types of things that were being practiced at that time. The conclusion from the wonderful creators of this document was that there was one single common denominator that had to do with being a physician, and it was caring. The ability to care. The structure of medical education right now had nothing to do with that, and it essentially needed to be completely revamped. Students did not need to be taught fact after fact, because they were in the process of change.

They needed to learn how to access those facts with modern technology, and they needed to learn something about caring and about inner personal skills. Well, unfortunately, there have been some problems in adopting all those suggestions because of the financial crises that some of the medical schools are in right now. But I saw a glimmer of hope there that I did not plan to see in my lifetime.

Sometimes we think the way it is now is the way it's always been. One of the things that struck me in Imagery and Healing *was your reference to the Hippocratic Oath and Hippocrates and*

what that oath actually is—its inclusion of the Greek goddesses
of healing within the oath. I'd like to have you talk a little bit
about the history of how medicine changed to exclude the
shamanic approach, the nonrational approach.

I'm most familiar, of course, with the Western roots, which
we find in Greece. I think most people are unaware that the
Hippocratic Oath is a promise to the Greek gods and goddesses—
Aesclepius and his healing family— to practice healing in such a
way that's ethical and moral. Interestingly enough, though, the
major practice of medicine of Aesclepius and his family, had to
do with imagery. They were actually treating those patients that
were given up in an era where medicine was at a very high point.
Surgery and pharmacology had reached a peak, and yet when
those patients could not be cured by those means, they would go
to Aesclepian temples, be advised to think good thoughts, to doze
off, and Aesclepius or a representative of Aesclepius would then
come down from his throne. During this twilight state, they
would get advice on the diagnosis and often information on the
cure. It's precisely what we're doing now in a more modern setting—using the imagination.

From that time, medicine, because of the political, economic, and social situation in Europe, began a nosedive that it did not
recover from until about 150 years ago. Well, perhaps 200 years
ago. A lot of it had to do with the fact that Christianity was
sweeping the country. The respect and love for the body that the
Greeks felt was no longer there. The body was scorned—hair
shirts, ashes, flagellation. All of those things were attempts to
show that the body was really not the important thing in this life.
During that era, though, there was a thread of healing that had to
do with the practice of women that I've become very interested
in. They, in truth, didn't nurture only their families, but there was
apparently an oral tradition of herbology, of anatomy, of all of the
things that we have put into our modern medical bag were passed

on from generation to generation—probably through women.

Even Paracelsus, who is regarded as the founder of modern chemistry, threw out the books that he was using—this was in the early Renaissance period. He threw out the canon, threw out the other bibles of medicine, and went to the wise women. Paracelsus was not highly popular, because in order to move in that direction, what was needed were naturalistic intuitive processes. Well, who was practicing these things? Normally, the women. They were giving their services very cheaply. Their efforts, even at midwifery, were regarded as somewhat of a competition, and there's some pretty good documentation of that. This element of healing we assumed was effective because it was indeed a threat for those who were attempting to establish a medical lineage. The women were classified in various ways as witches. There are reports that approximately nine million of them were burned. Certainly they were not all practicing healing. Certainly they were not all witches. Nevertheless, being declared a healer was sufficient cause for execution in some places.

It's incredible. There were a lot less people then, too.

A lot less people, and some villages ended up with one or two women apiece. In reading this, one has to sit back and ask, "Why?" Yet it was regarded as necessary for the continuation of development of both religion and science. It is that yoke that we are currently living under, In terms of scientific medicine and of attempting to keep out the intuitive, the nonrational, the nurturing mode that since recorded time with medicine has been regarded as healing.

Now, one of the ways imaging has kind of integrated itself into mainstream medicine is through the use of technology— namely, biofeedback. Could you talk a little bit about that, because I know you're experienced in biofeedback technology.

Biofeedback is recognized by main-line medicine, and most insurance companies will pay for it. It is now regarded as something that not only works, but is cost effective. My interest in biofeedback and my knowledge of it tells me that it is simply an imagery trainer. The machines in and of themselves do nothing and, in fact, are not necessary. If you want to take the time, you can become sensitive to the physiological and the psychological cues you get, but we typically do not want to do that. We don't have the time to sit in a cave and do deep breathing exercises for seven years, and biofeedback is a remarkable substitute, a palatable substitute.

What's interesting is that biofeedback has achieved its acceptance in a relatively brief span of time. I mean, I can think of 15 years ago, biofeedback was out there on the leading edge. It was far out, and now it's accepted. That's a short time.

It is a short time. What that tells me is that we should have a real celebration of the power of the technique, number one. But, in truth, the ability that people have once they've been given a little bit of information—no matter how crude it is—is that they then are able to go on and alter the physiology in some remarkable ways. We can do anything with ourselves provided we're given enough information. Some of our frustration in this work is that the technology is not ready yet for some of the things that we want to do.

For example, if, in fact, we could have constant monitoring of our immune system, there's every reason to believe that we could alter the components of that immune system, and when that becomes possible, we have then dealt with virtually every major puzzling crippler and killer of this society, this civilization. What we found, though, is that for those things that cannot yet be monitored, like the immune system, there are some control trials showing that imagery process is sufficient. We really don't need the feedback from machines. If we go through a series of tried-and-true procedures that sound suspiciously like what Aesclepius was doing, then we're able to manipulate various components of our immune system.

How has your work with imaging and the imagination helped you? How have you interacted with it personally? You've written some books and you've been doing your research and so forth, but how has it affected your own life?

I think perhaps I'm cancer phobic. Everybody in my family who has died has died of cancer. So a lot of my work may have come out of that phobia. I don't have that particularly anymore. I have demonstrated to myself that I've reversed some conditions of my own that have let me know that I'm on the right track. Nothing serious, but tests, anyway, of my own belief system. When I use the imagery process in my own life, it always works. When I don't use it, it does not work. It's like any other medicine. If I use it to plan my day, if I sit down and image my goals, image my relationships that I need to establish with other people, see myself moving in a direction that feels good for me, then the day goes well. When I don't do that, it doesn't go particularly well.

I'm really glad that you mentioned that, because I think, again, we get a bias toward, well, we only use imaging when we've got a problem, a health problem. Actually, you can use imaging for a lot of things.

Absolutely. That's what happens to the patients I work with. They'll use it for their health problem, overcome their health problem, then find out that imagery is a really great gift. It's a way that they can prepare themselves for examinations—for competition, sports competition. Just for general living. It's a way of rehearsing situations before they happen so that you can perform at your best. This is not new stuff. This is in the sports literature and every other kind of thing. It's important because it creates the methods that people use to heal themselves, to do a daily surveillance. Say, wait a second now, I feel tightness here, something is wrong here. There's a lump in my throat. Have I swallowed too many words or gotten myself into a situation that I don't want to be in? So it's used in a preventive sense, also, as well as kind of a planning mental rehearsal way.

But you find that you use imaging a lot in your own daily life.

Absolutely. I woke up one morning and realized that I've been under a great deal of stress for two years and that I realigned my whole jaw. It was going to be a very costly procedure. Two years of braces and restructuring, and what that told me is that I'd been kidding myself for a couple years. Now I'm working not only with my own imagery process, but with some dentists, some orthodontists. Also, what's created, of course, is a re-examination of how I managed to hide that stress from myself. I simply did not believe that I would take it out on my jaw. I was looking perfectly healthy all this time, as far as I was concerned. No infectious disease, my heart worked, my blood pressure wasn't too bad, yet everybody's body is a subtle reminder. I often entertain the idea that if we were truly on our paths, if we knew the answer to where we needed to go, we wouldn't need a body. It's like knocking on the door of the psyche constantly. When you don't listen to it, it knocks harder and harder.

What do you see as the future of imaging and its relationship to modern medicine and contemporary medicine? And the change that really obviously needs to happen. How do you see it happening?

What's happening now is absolutely necessary to happen to allow concepts like imagery to get back where they belong, which is in the treatment of people who are suffering. The study must be good to come out of someplace like Harvard, regardless of the results. If the results are negative or if they're positive, then we'll interpret them as they come, but this is what must happen.

Besides reading some of the literature, what would be some advice you might give to readers who would be interested in pursuing imaging and learning more about it? What would be something that they could do?

Contact the American Imagery Institute at Marquette, and the Academy of Guided Imagery in Mill Valley, California. Frank and I do one-year certification programs that meet four times a year for intensive work. Read books on imagery and hypnosis (rituals). My new book, *Rituals of Healing,* is full of simple self-help exercises. There's a lot of literature available. There's literature for the person who does not particularly want a scientific orientation but who wants exercises.

What about churches that use imagery as part of their teaching?

The New Thought churches such as Unity Church of Religious Science became popular at the turn of the century. I became interested in those churches because many of them were founded by women, and they have a healing tradition. One of the threads that I kept identifying throughout the healing work was that when the religious base for a culture was androgynous or female, then women were healers. Emerging during this Victorian and post-Victorian era were all sorts of articulate women who founded their churches, used a lot of visualization and imagery in healing, and they had a brief, bright moment there.

Well, I also think of Mary Baker Eddy, creator of Christian Science, who was heavily influenced by the philosophy of the East.

She did, indeed. Looking at her philosophy, it is not a whole lot different from what we've developed in terms of what we think as a more scientific type of imagery. The Christian Scientists don't go along very well with our methods because of their belief that you must visualize yourself pure and whole. We're saying confront the problem, confront the pain. Look at it, get into it, become part of it. Understand your enemy, and then the fight can ensue, which is a very different position.

Yes, I think that's a very interesting point you're making. You have to have an understanding. It's not just positive thinking that we're talking about here. I think so often we miss that. We think we're just talking about positive thinking, but we're not. We're really talking about having to understand the process and understand the nature of what it is we're dealing with in order to make the visualization or the imaging work.

Exactly. I did a call-in talk show sometime ago, and a woman called in from another part of California. She said, "You know, I do think positively, and I'm still sick." That's exactly the point. There's no easy answer. There's nothing that one can image or visualize that's going to necessarily change the state of their lives.

It's as if one has to go through the process and learn the material in order to let go of it. But if you just try to let go of it without learning it, you can't do it. An interesting paradox that we have there.

It seems to me that there are so many things that are attainable if we just open up to the possibilities we have available with-

in our capacity. Imaging is just one of them. It's certainly an important one that so often is forgotten.

One of the things I need to keep in mind, too, is that the scientific method that has stood the test of time may not be the appropriate way to look at some of these issues. In fact, I'm getting a great distrust of what does come out of the scientific method. I can say that as someone who teaches research design every single year. There are other ways of knowing and establishing the reliability of some of the things we feel. We must allow ourselves that as legitimate data. In the history of medicine, the early scientific researchers tested everything on themselves. Drugs were calibrated on physicians, which, of course, led to some significant problems, but this was the way. This was all there was. Intuition, listening to one's own response to various treatments that were being proposed—this was the accepted way in the past.

Actually, we have to go back to the roots of science instead of taking the modern scientific approach, which has just been developed in the last few hundred years. Those roots of science are certainly in our life experience. And what works and what doesn't work—we've lost that in some respects.

EPILOGUE

"The image is the world's oldest and greatest healing resource," maintains Jeanne Achterberg, who has spent the past two decades studying the power of imagination as a tool in health, healing, and the quest for mind/body/spirit wholeness. Being able to visualize and use our intuition abilities provides us with yet another tool to learn the spiritual dimensions of our own being. Imagery is the gateway to the depths of inner experience and outer expression. Seeing through the mind's eye can open us to the life of the soul where all things are possible and life becomes one timeless continuum.

As we take time in our daily life to meditate and pray, we can use the power of the imagination and intuition to support and build upon our inner experience. The clearest pictures we see are those we create inside ourselves. This is why the great spiritual traditions place such emphasis on silence and solitude. Many of the intricate thangkas of Tibetan Buddhism, with their multiple images and elaborate design elements, were inspired by the inner visualization of some great yogi in the past. Now, the revealed imagery is used as a focal point for meditative practice and for self-discovery. The clear implication is that we can return from the territory of the inner being with treasures that will help us in our everyday life. Such is the innate power of healing imagery.

CHAPTER EIGHT

A CONSCIOUS APPROACH TO BREATHING

Gay Hendricks, with Shoshana Alexander

(Shoshana Alexander is a New Dimensions interviewer who works with Michael Toms.)

PROLOGUE

*T*hroughout thousands of years of human history, breath has been recognized as a vehicle for healing and transcendence. *Breathing is perhaps the most intimate and essential action of our lives. Yet many of us give it little thought or regard. Few of us, in fact, get beyond childhood still capable of breathing fully and naturally. In the traumas and stresses of our lives, we abandon the one simple tool that can carry us through to healing. Rediscovering our birthright of healthy breathing is just a breath* *away, a conscious breath. That is our focus today. Consciously retraining and deepening our awareness of our breathing, we can bring about dramatic changes in our lives. From relieving headaches to eliminating depression and anxiety. From alleviating diseases and addictions to improving our performance levels. From deepening our relationships to discovering a bridge to the divine. Gay Hendricks, a pioneer in breath work and body-centered therapies, is the author (and co-author), along with his wife, Kathlyn Hendricks, of over 20 books in psychology and education. Among them are* Learning to Love Yourself, At the Speed of Life, Conscious Loving, *and the focus of this interview,* Conscious Breathing. *Gay received his Ph.D. from Stanford in 1974 and is a professor of counseling at the University of Colorado. He and Kathlyn conduct workshops nationwide and run the Hendricks Institute in Santa Barbara.*

SHOSHANA ALEXANDER: *Gay, learning how to breathe consciously basically saved your life. Would you tell us something of that story—how you realized you weren't really breathing and how you came to understand what conscious breathing is?*

GAY HENDRICKS: Yes. I was living in New England, and I could honestly say that I never thought about breathing before in my whole life. I was working on my master's degree in counseling, but it was very cognitively oriented. This fit me perfectly, because here I was, I weighed 300 pounds, I was smoking two or three packs of Marlboros a day, I was in a very troubled marriage at the time, and I was walking out in the woods one day, and I slipped on the ice. I smashed the back of my head on the ice. As I went down through the layers of unconsciousness, I had the experience of going down through the layers of myself and seeing that I was, at my essence, absolutely pure and conscious. Yet

I had all these levels of unexplored feelings and body tensions wrapped around that pure essence. So it was a moment for me of seeing myself as I really was, and then as I came back into consciousness, it was as if I assembled all of those layers of who I *wasn't* on top of that pure essence.

What I noticed in that moment is that my breathing had changed. It was totally free and open and easy. It was not restricted like it was when I was living in my normal life. It took a whack on the back of my head to actually open myself up to the real truth of who I was. Now I can get down to that level easily after 20-some years of meditation and breath work without hitting myself on the head. But in those days, I think I was so thick that it took that whack on the back of my head to really wake me up. Fortunately, I woke up in time and began to explore my feelings and unwind my body tensions and learn to use my breath as a searchlight for going down through the middle of my self to the very core. I guess what I really learned in that moment was that my breathing was a vehicle for transcendence of myself and the exploration of the deepest level of myself. Then I began to use it with clients to help them explore themselves.

You talk about discovering this breath work, in some sort of way, tripping into it, before you even knew about it.

Absolutely. In fact, I'm glad it happened that way, because so much of education is involved with things that you later have to unlearn. I'm glad I didn't have to unlearn anybody else's approach to breath work. What I did was simply take it on as an experimental process in myself. I began to ask myself the questions that, had there been a teacher around, I would have asked him or her. But there was no teacher around in those days of breath work, so I just had to experiment with it myself. I'm so glad I did, because I now know cell things—things that had I had a teacher tell them to me, I might not have actually experimented with them until I knew them deep down to my cells.

It seems interesting to actually have that kind of insight and intuition. You talk about the wife of a colleague coming into your office, and she was filled with fear and anxiety. You didn't really know what to do, and yet you found yourself doing something that many therapists use now. Would you talk about that story?

It was really the moment for me when I first saw with my own two eyes the power of breath work. The woman was feeling a lot of anger. She was angry about an affair that her husband was having. As is often the case with anger, the roots of anger are really in fear. Most people don't realize this, but when they're angry, it's really something you're scared about. If you stay angry about it, that keeps you away from actually confronting what you're scared about. I began to use that idea with her. I asked her to look underneath the anger and find out what she was really afraid of.

She began to talk about what she was afraid of, and I noticed that her breathing changed. First it changed, in a sense, for the worse, because she kept holding her breath as she spoke. She would say a sentence and then go [breath] and kind of hold the in-breath, and then she would say another sentence and [breath]. So I said, "Instead of doing that, holding your breath, go ahead and take full free breaths and breathe into your fear. Instead of trying to get away from your fear and get rid of it, actually go ahead and experience it. Surrender yourself to it. Let's just treat it as another sacred aspect of life. Just go ahead and be with it, participate with it."

As she began to do this, her breathing got deeper and deeper. Within 15 minutes or so, she had completely eliminated the fear and anger from her body by breathing through it. At the end of that time, at the end of that 15 or 20 minutes, she looked radiant. She looked reborn. She looked absolutely as different than when she had first come in the door as you could possibly imagine.

Then the most amazing thing happened. Without my even asking her the questions, she thought up a number of creative solutions to the problem with her husband—including one, which neither one of us had thought of. It was simply telling him the truth of her feelings. How she felt about it. That's often the last thing we think of.

The experience showed me that at the bottom of everything we do, we have an organic ability to come up with our own solutions to things. We are totally creative beings. It's just that we don't get to that level oftentimes because we don't participate deeply enough with what's actually going on in ourselves. There's a wonderful line from James Joyce where he says that Mr. Duffy lives a short distance from his body. Isn't that the truth about how often we keep ourselves one step removed from fully participating with our feelings, from fully participating with our organic creativity.

What you've found is that breath is the avenue into those answers, as that woman discovered, into all of our answers— whether it's the physical, emotional, spiritual, or mental.

One of my favorite quotes that goes along with that is from Fritz Perls, the founder of Gestalt therapy. He said fear is excitement without the breath—the very same feeling that if we breathed into it would be excitement. It would actually catapult us into creative action, but we hold our breath, and that turns into fear, and it turns into an emotion that can actually help strangle us rather than free us into our creativity.

You've been working now for the last 20 years basically researching breath work and developing body-centered therapies. In your latest book, Conscious Breathing, *you added a subtitle:* Breath Work for Health, Stress Release, and Personal Mastery. *It's quite a spectrum.*

Yes. It really is. Breath has that power. It can be something you can use in three seconds. Oftentimes, if you were watching me in my office with a client, you'd see me do something that just took a matter of seconds. A person is feeling sad, and I'll say, "Go ahead, take a few breaths into that. Just go ahead and open up into that sadness." It may take five seconds, or you could spend an entire lifetime going for transcendence through your breathing like many yogis may have done.

What is conscious breathing, in the way that you're using that term?

Conscious breathing is the intended use of breathing as a vehicle for opening up your consciousness so that you choose to do certain breathing activities or practices with a conscious intention of opening up to learn more about yourself—to open up, to experience yourself more deeply, with the ultimate aim of uncovering your own organic spirituality and your own organic creativity.

In your book, Conscious Breathing, *you talk about the fact that so many people are upside-down breathers or shallow breathers. How would a person know if he or she is that kind of breather or if one is not breathing fully? What could someone do to correct it?*

There really is one universal breathing problem. It can be summarized as follows. Upside-down breathing, what we call upside-down breathing, is when you breathe in and tighten your stomach muscles so that the breath goes up into the chest. It's a common reaction when children are scared, for example. You'll notice that they'll tighten their belly muscles and breathe up high in the chest. They'll take a big in-breath and hold a big breath up in the chest.

The universal breathing problem really involves tightening in the very place where you should relax in order to let a full breath go deep down into your stomach, down into your belly. When we're in the grip of fear, we tighten our stomach muscles and throw a big breath up into the chest. That actually has the effect of flooding our body with adrenaline, which a hundred thousand years ago worked great. We had tigers to escape from and other cave persons to throw rocks at and that kind of thing. In today's environment, we're usually not in a position where we're escaping from a predator or throwing a rock at a saber-toothed tiger. What we have now are social situations where it's really not appropriate to fight back or to run out of the room. That's the power of breathing. Take big, deep, slow belly breaths so that your whole body gets nurtured with breath.

Can you give us some instructions for conscious breathing?

I'd like everybody in the world to know how to take a full diaphragmatic breath. The reason the diaphragm is so important is if it doesn't move through its full range of motion, it leaves too much carbon dioxide in our bodies, and it puts us ill at ease. If you use your diaphragm fully, then your body is cleaned out with each breath. Many of our toxins are released through the breath. A very small percentage are actually released through the skin or other parts of the body, but the body is designed to release most of its toxins out of the breath.

You can experiment wherever you are with this. The first thing to do is to find out what having tight stomach muscles feels like. That's really a key to learning to relax them. First, tighten and relax your stomach muscles several times. If your hands are free where you could actually feel them, put your hand about halfway between your belly button and the top of your pubic bone, your lower abdomen. Tighten those muscles a few times and relax them, so that you really get a sense of what the difference is between having your muscles relaxed and having them tightened. The crucial thing in healthy breath is to relax those muscles on the in-breath so that your breath goes down and in and makes your belly round slightly with the in-breath. Then on the out-breath, to breathe out completely, so you breathe right to the very last drop of your breath. Then to relax those stomach muscles and take that full belly breath way deep down into the stomach so that the belly rounds with each in-breath.

When you're breathing correctly, you don't have to worry too much about getting breath up into your chest. It'll take care of itself. You want to aim the breath down and in so that it really rounds that area between your navel and the top of your pubic bone. That's the key area you want to keep softening in order to get a full breath down in there. Everybody, all day long, can mix themselves what I call an oxygen cocktail right there on the spot by taking a nice deep belly breath. I do it all the time in meetings. You know like sometimes I'll have to sit at a boring meeting for a couple of hours, and afterwards, friends and colleagues will often say something like, "Gee, you had a smile on your face throughout that whole meeting. Why was that?" I'd say, "Well, I was just practicing my breath work."

What about the medical study that points out that 75 percent of diseases are due to poor breathing?

There have been several studies that have indicated that—the main one being a very creative study in which a graduate student sat in a medical doctor's office and simply asked him to watch breathing patterns in the waiting room. He found that over 80 percent of the people in the waiting room had disturbed breathing. Regardless of what their physical problem was, they had disturbed breathing patterns. That was one of the most fascinating things I've ever read. Here's a situation where none of those people were probably going to go in there and have anything dealt with about their breathing. Many of the most creative medical doctors I know suggest looking at breathing along with everything else. Many medical doctors say disturbed breathing goes along with illness, but which one of them comes first? We're not sure. You know that it could be that the disturbed breathing actually creates the situation in which there's a disturbance in other organs in the body.

Have you worked with people with asthma? Addictions? Major anxieties? Depressions?

Yes. Being a psychologist, I found that most of the use of the work that I do involves learning how to be with our emotions in a healthier way—learning how to breathe with our feelings rather than hold our breath against them. We have worked with hundreds of cases of asthma, allergies, and other kinds of things like headaches that people perhaps sought conventional medical treatment for. They tried drugs, they tried allopathic medicine, and they hadn't worked. We treat them with very simple breathing practices just like the kind that we have illustrated in the book. We find very, very powerful results and increased physical health. In fact, we have a kind of a standing thing that we tell our breathing students. We say do this ten-minute daily breathing program every day for a year, and you won't have any of the problems you came in with today. It's kind of a radical statement, but we have yet to have anybody come back and say, "Hey, that didn't work." So we're very proud of that.

I'm wondering how something so simple can be so overlooked.

I think it's because so many of us growing up as children have healthy breathing traumatized out of us. Often we're subject to emotional traumas or physical injuries that actually cause a disturbance in breathing processes. In one famous osteopathic study, Dr. Vial Lafryman examined 1,250 newborns about six to nine months after their birth. She found that about 750 of them had some kind of disturbance of their breathing process that happened as a result of the birth process itself. Oftentimes, birth can be very hazardous to our health, and sometimes people don't recover from insults to the breath caused by some kind of disturbance at birth for many, many years. Sometimes it starts very early on.

You did your own study of 100 babies and found that virtually all of them breathed fully into their bellies.

When I went looking for a hundred healthy babies, it took me more than a hundred to find a hundred babies who had undisturbed breathing processes. When I decide to study a subject, I do my best to start from the ground up. I want to start by looking at what's healthy, because in psychology we focus so much on ill health that we don't often focus on what "normal" should look like.

I went out and found healthy babies and just watched the way they breathed. I based most of my breathing program on what I learned from these three-month-old, five-month-old infants. I also did a lot of studying of animals to find out what healthy animal breathing looked like and even watched amoebae. I learned from very young life forms what breathing should be like before traumas interfere later on.

You point out, however, that by the time most children are in the sixth grade in our culture, they no longer breathe properly. You say also that in urban environments, people breathe more shallowly. I find that when a car goes by, I tend to breathe more shallowly. There's kind of a fear to take those pollutants into the body. Should we really not fully breathe the pollutants around us?

I think your body is probably doing a very wise thing. If a bus goes past you when you're riding your bicycle or walking and the air is full of diesel fuel, for certain you want to avoid getting those in your body. I find that happens a lot on airplanes, too—there are a lot of pollutants that circulate in the airplane air. I notice I'll be breathing more shallowly to keep from taking those into my body. I think that is a natural self-protective mechanism. Also, the oxygen level around cities is quite a bit lower than it is elsewhere. On the earth itself now, the oxygen level is somewhere 21 or 23 percent, something like that, down from about 30-some percent when the earth was first formed. Around cities it's even less, the actual level of oxygen in the air. If you're going out jogging or bike riding on a smoggy day, definitely use some kind of filter. Put a bandana around your nose, or buy some filters from a bike store that you can use to help filter out some of the larger pollutants out of the air. It is a very wise thing to do in today's polluted environment.

So there are times when it's good not to breathe deeply. Most of the time you're saying that breathing is the way through to healing, and you use this with emotions. You talk about how we can breathe through the emotion. Can you explain about breath and emotion?

One of the problems is that unless we know how to breathe correctly, unless we take full diaphragmatic belly breaths, emotions can actually stay locked in our bodies. If you try to control an emotion like fear by holding your breath then tightening up against it, it doesn't get rid of it. It just means that it's going to live at a subconscious level for a while in your body. In other words, it's going to drop down beneath the level of consciousness and just sit there.

In the cells? How does it live there?

It would appear that it does live at a physiological level in your cells. We notice in breath work sessions that we'll have a person take 15 or 20 big, healthy breaths, and suddenly they might burst into tears about something that happened when they were 7 or 8 years old. It's quite remarkable to see. The other use that I found of breathing is in helping to open up to and clear pain out of my body. Over the last seven or eight years now, I haven't used any kind of Novocaine at the dentist. I've waved off the nitrous oxide and waved off the big needle with the Novocaine in it and just used breathing.

The specific technique I use is simply to take full, deep, connected breaths and open up to the pain and sensation, rather than trying to close it down or get rid of it. I open up and participate with it fully. The fascinating paradox is the more I open up and participate with the pain, then it doesn't seem like pain anymore. It stops being pain and simply becomes sensation. I once was the breathing coach at a birth, and my client was practicing breathing when I went out of the room. When I came back, I said, "Do you have any pain?" She said, "No, I've just got sensation now." She was taking these big, deep, full breaths. She transformed the pain into pure sensation. So it let me know that pain in a way is partly a judgment by our minds that comes up as a result of resisting the actual sensations. If we can participate with them fully and honor them and love them and appreciate them and learn from them, then it becomes not painful, but just simply more of life.

Any of our readers who have sat in meditation cross-legged or even in a chair for a long period of time might have experienced that same thing. The meditators are often encouraged to just remain, observing. You have studied vipassana. Is there a link between what you do and these ancient Buddhist teachings?

I believe that almost everything that we use nowadays are probably things that the ancient yogis and meditators used four or five thousand years ago during the great spiritual flowering in India and Thailand and places like that. I've found that the principles of meditation, whether it's vipassana or transcendental meditation or zen meditation, are really the principles of good living and good breathing. What all good meditation says is participate with what is. Feel it deeply. Be with it. Don't resist it. Let yourself experience it, and then it becomes something that's a pure process of life. It's not something to be resisted or judged or made right or made wrong. It's simply what is, and that's what we need to put our attention on. With our breath or with our consciousness, simply participating with the way things are.

If someone is using their breath to breathe through tiredness or depression or even physical pain, is there any danger that perhaps they might not be using the message that that tiredness is giving—that they need rest? Or not using the message that the anxiety or the physical pain is giving them? Could you breathe through those things mistakenly?

I believe that it works a little bit differently than that. I believe that actually participating with something, with your breath and with your consciousness, feeling it, breathing through it, will lead you to action quicker. I found that if I breathe through my fear suddenly, the action I need to take is revealed to me very quickly. Whereas if I don't, if I resist that, it may take me longer to get to the actual message of it. I've not actually found it to be true that people avoid taking action by participating with things and breathing through things. I found that it actually catapults them into action quicker.

For instance, if people are tired and they breathe through that tiredness, the message they may get is, Oh, I need to sleep.

That's right, you may get a message like that. It's a very valuable thing, but at the time they may not be in a place where they could actually lie down and rest. They might be driving their car at three o'clock in the morning, and they need to get through that last half hour or 45 minutes to actually take the effective action.

Something more on emotions. Is it safe for anyone, any reader at home, to use this deep breathing into the belly to breathe through emotions that come up?

I would say that if you have any doubt, get yourself a guide. We are talking about very gentle things that are always done in the comfort zone. As long as you stay in the zone of comfort, that's what we're looking for. There may be situations where you might want to get yourself a therapist or a breath worker or a guide to help you breathe in some kind of intense, deep way. In that situation, I would recommend doing it with a guide, with a helper, rather than trying to do it on your own. I think, practically speaking, what I've noticed that people have reported to me is that they try to do things on their own, and they'll stop halfway through it without going the rest of the way through. That's where your guide or doctor or your helper could give you a nudge to go all the way through and complete it.

You talk about feelings having a rhythm, a beginning, a middle, and an end.

For example, I was working with a person who began sobbing very deeply about certain things that happened in her childhood. As I began to encourage her to breathe with that and to let herself actually feel that emotion even more deeply, after a few minutes she sobbed into an even deeper level of sadness that she identified as being a collective level of sadness of all of the women in her lineage who had felt pain that they didn't know how to deal with. She broke through from the personal level to a deeper, more collective level of sadness. Once she let that come through and breathe through that, she came out of that feeling absolutely radiant. But I don't think she would've gotten through that unless she used her breath to go through to that deeper, more collective level. It wasn't just about her life. It was about her whole lineage and perhaps even the whole community of her gender that she was a repository of the feelings for.

The idea is to keep breathing, just trust the breathing, and trust the emotion itself.

Yes. It has everything you need right under your nose to teach you everything you need to know. It seems we need more people who will take enlightened social action, those who can breathe through their own pain and can help other people breathe through theirs. Then perhaps we can really turn our attention to taking actions that will elevate the level of consciousness for all concerned.

You are using the breath work in many different ways. We all need so much support when we're confronting major issues. One of the main areas you work with is with couples. What does breathing have to do with relationships?

Let me give you a very practical example. Oftentimes my wife and I, when we're doing work with a couple, will notice that when one person gets into an emotion, let's say anger or fear, the other person will hold his or her breath so that I might start feeling scared. You might hold your breath, in a sense, to try to control your feelings or to control my feelings. In couples' relationships, most of the problems are a struggle to control some energy or another. We try to control the other person, rather than simply opening a space for them to grow in whatever way they need to grow. We get into our own fear, and then we communicate to the other person in a way that keeps them stuck at a certain level.

Well, the problem in couples is often that struggle for control is really cutting down the life energy of everyone involved. How they do that, specifically, is often restricting their breathing. Elizabeth Browning said whoever breathes most air, lives most life. The idea being that if we really celebrate ourselves and open up to more deeper breathing and more healthy breathing, the more life we'll feel. We want to help couples stop trying to control each other and start trying to celebrate each other—particularly learning how to celebrate each other through their breathing, through meditating together, and through finding ways to really recognize the essence of the other person.

So couples can use breathing together, as well as individually?

Yes. We also use it in corporate settings with people who need to function in the corporate environment, which is often a very hostile place to learn how to keep your essence alive.

Besides using breath work for curing diseases and addictions, tensions, stresses, you also say something that is really significant. You talk about the fact that there are no upper limits to how good you can feel. You talk about expanding, extending that sense, that capacity for well-being.

Yes. One thing that I caught on to early on is what in some of our other books we call "the upper limits problem." People have a thermostat setting, in a sense, on how much positive energy they can feel. Their belief system is such that they don't allow themselves to feel very good before they bring themselves back down with some kind of unpleasant or negative event. We've had literally hundreds, probably thousands, of people tell us that when they come into therapy, they had something bad happen to them right after a period of feeling good. We began to catch on years ago with couples that they didn't fight after a period of feeling bad. They often started a fight right after a period of feeling good.

So one reason we began to use breathing so much was to help people actually expand their capacity to feel good. We would have them breathe, take 10 or 12 deep breaths, and then just rest and let themselves feel good. Some of the activities that are in the book are based on this principle. You want to stay in your comfort zone. Take 10 or 12 big deep breaths, and then rest in that positive energy. Instead of having something bad happen, let's go expand in positive energy and then rest. Expand some more, and then rest, instead of expand, contract, expand, contract. So we want to learn to heal the upper limits problem by allowing ourselves to feel expanding waves of positive energy and letting ourselves rest and be comfortable in that positive energy. See, human beings know a great deal about how to feel bad. We've been doing it for centuries and centuries and centuries. What we don't know yet is how to organically feel good for long periods of time. We need to kind of grow these new positive energy channels in ourselves so that we can actually learn to experience higher and higher levels of organic bliss and organic good feelings.

How is it that the breath can be expanding in that way? How can breath enhance that capacity?

On a purely physiological level, if you learn how to breathe deeper and more powerfully, as with exercise, you actually grow more capillary space in your body. For example, there are about 60,000 miles of capillary space in your body. But if you're a regular exerciser, you have a lot more than that. You may have another 10- or 20,000 miles of capillary space in your body. You've literally got more space for feeling in your body. Good breathing also enhances that ability to grow a larger version of yourself, even on a purely physiological level.

After 20 years, you must have expanded to 20,000 miles at least.

As a matter of fact, I recently had my breathing capacity tested. I have the breathing capacity of a 19-year-old, 6'6", 240-pound boy. It felt really good because I just had my 50th birthday, and it really felt good to know that I'm at least breathing like a 19-year-old. I may not look like a 19-year-old, but my breathing is that way.

Do you find that through this conscious breathing you can actually stay in a state of well-being?

I've found that actually from my own life. I used to be quite a moody person. Ups and downs. Ups and downs. Bad moods, the lot, and everything. The number-one thing that I've noticed in my life is that mood swings have totally disappeared. Basically, I stay in a good mood all the time, and it has been since I learned how to breathe. I think that in the old days, my mood swings were largely a function of not knowing how to breathe. Once I learned how to breathe and got that good, steady energy flowing in my body, I just didn't fluctuate around as much as I did. I've certainly noticed that now with hundreds, perhaps even thousands, of other clients that have studied the program.

The idea that there is a rhythm to everything, there is day and night, positive and negative, need not necessarily mean that we have to go into depression in order to balance out our high points?

No. As a matter of fact, what I have found with depression is that oftentimes depression is the result of a long period of not listening to some feeling. Not listening to your anger. Or not listening to your fear. After a while, you get kind of burnt out by resisting the message that's trying to come into your self through your emotions. We teach people to breathe with and acknowledge and listen to their emotions, rather than trying to drown them out.

When they do that, their moods often improve radically, very quickly.

You present these techniques for breathing in a very simple way. It's a very simple process, yet something profound is going on here. Where is all this going? What is it that you'd really like to be conveying to our readers?

My wife, Kathlyn, and I have done quite a bit of thinking at our institute about what our goals are and what our purposes are. We really narrowed them down to three things, which are very simple, yet have far-ranging consequences. The first thing is that we really want to teach people a way to live in harmony inside their bodies. Breathing can do that. The second thing we want to teach people is how to live in harmony in their relationships. We've developed a very simple way of communicating and breathing together so that people in relationship can really achieve harmony. The third thing we're very interested in is creating harmony in the larger community.

In the ancient Hawaiian language, for example, the word *ohana* means "family," and it also means "people who breathe together." Our ultimate vision is planetary healing through people who have learned how to experience their inner harmony, and relationship harmony using these very powerful, simple, organic things like breathing and meditation.

Would you say that the essence of life is harmony and love, and that through our breathing, we can follow an avenue into that?

I would agree with that completely. I have personally experienced that, to my own radical amazement, and that's what I would wish for everybody on this planet: to learn how to open up and discover these simple paths to their own harmony and to their creative expression. I think one of the greatest sources of pain on this planet is people's unexpressed creativity. I want very much to help people learn how to go down through that and find their way of expressing their full creative potential using their own simple, organic, natural gifts.

EPILOGUE

Through the breath comes life. The Latin word for "breath" is *spiritus,* from which we take the word, *spirit.* The Latin for "breathe in" is the word *inspirare.* Inspiration then is, literally, to breathe in the spirit. It is clear that there is a direct relationship between the breath, life, and the spirit. Any path to wholeness of mind/body/spirit must necessarily integrate learning to breathe properly. This is why so often instruction in basic meditation practice begins with paying attention to the breath. The key to successful meditation is the proper manipulation of the breath. I think breathing naturally and feeling relaxed are also important components for prayer.

Just taking a few minutes in the midst of a busy day to focus on breathing can make all the difference in how you experience what goes on around you. A few deep breaths can help relax and energize you and serve as a reminder of what's really important, as life passes by like a speeding train. Through the breath, you can stay centered in the middle of the maelstrom and be confident of getting the most from each moment.

CHAPTER NINE

A DIALOGUE ABOUT
CONVERSATIONS
WITH GOD

Neale Donald Walsch, with Michael Toms

PROLOGUE

*I*t occurs to me that most people reading this book have probably imagined what it might be like to have a conversation with
God. Would He or She pay attention? If God heard me, would I
receive an answer? How would I know? These are soulful queries
that any of us may have pondered at different points in our life.
Perhaps God speaks to us all the time, and we just don't know
how to listen. Neale Donald Walsch stopped, listened, and tran-
scribed what he heard. It evolved into a book entitled
Conversations with God: An Uncommon Dialogue. *Neale lives
with his wife, Nancy, in southern Oregon. Together they have*

formed ReCreation, an organization whose goal is to give people back to themselves. Walsch tours the country lecturing and hosting workshops, and spreading the messages contained in Conversations with God.

MICHAEL TOMS: *Neale, I'd like to go back to earlier times. What led you to start writing the book that became* Conversations with God*? Where were you at that time? What was life like?*

NEALE DONALD WALSCH: I think I was at the *nadir* of my existence—a word I never knew existed until Spiro Agnew used it many years ago. The lowest point, really, of my life. Relative to other people's lives, my life wasn't so horrible, but it simply wasn't at all what I thought it would be. My relationships—all of them, really—with my significant others were not working. My career was terribly unrewarding, very unfulfilling. Even my health, quite predictably, was not good. I was very frustrated during this period of time, which was in the early part of 1992. I was very, very upset—upset with myself, upset with others in my life who I thought were doing it to me. But most of all, I was really upset with life itself. Upset with the universe. Upset with God, I suppose—very, very angry, because I thought that I had played by the rules.

I did what my father and my mother told me I ought to do to make life work, and I was rapidly approaching my 50th year, but none of it was falling into place. I didn't have anything to show for my nearly half-century on the planet. I didn't own a home. I was barely able to afford the rent on the place that I was renting. I had very little in material acquisitions. Not that I really measured my idea of success in material acquisitions, but I had literally nothing. I think it was midlife crisis in a huge way. In a very big way. I fell into a period of what I almost want to call chronic depression for a number of months. Four or five months feeling very, very down about everything. Again, I want to emphasize that I understand that everything is relative. Life is all relative. Relative to other people's existence on this planet, I was in heaven. You look across the ocean at people, the way people live in other countries, and you have to appreciate that I was living a wonderful life. But relative to where I thought I would be at the age of 50, nothing was falling into place. The worst part about it was that I was so desperately unhappy in my personal relationships with everyone, and my relationship with God—what I imagined to be God.

Were you raised in a particular religion? Did you have a religious background?

I was raised a Roman Catholic, born and raised in the Roman Catholic church. I had a very religious upbringing, very religious background. I was given at a very early age a deep sense that there was something else going on here, a much larger experience, and that there were larger realities. I had a very clear understanding that there was a thing, however we wanted to define it, that we called God. So I believed in God. I think surveys have shown that almost 90 percent of the people in the world believe in God in some form or another. It's a remarkable number. I was one of those people who believed in God, although I didn't have much of an idea about it beyond that. I just thought there was one, but I did have a Roman Catholic background and upbringing. I left the Church, as they say, in my late teens.

Did you explore any other religions? What happened?

I explored every other religion there is, or just about. From the time I was a very young child, from the age of six or seven or eight, I was transfixed with the idea of God. I know I prayed to God in a very personal way. I can recall being seven and eight years old, talking to God the way I'm talking to you. That was not so common among seven- and eight-year-olds in my time. I always had or imagined myself to have this very personal relationship with God. But as I grew older, God was presented to me in all of the configurations, with all the dogma surrounding Him, by the Roman Catholic church. I mean this with no disrespect to the Catholic church. Simply that they surrounded God with so much dogma that I found myself not comfortable within that paradigm.

I began exploring, to answer your question, virtually every other religion that I could explore. I looked at Protestantism. I looked at Lutheranism. I looked at Judaism. I looked at everything, really. I started looking at many of the religious constructions of the Far East over a period of many years, beginning with forays into the library and ending with some very sophisticated talks that I wound up having with members of the clergy from all those faiths. In fact, in one of my moments of great imagination, I invited ministers from every faith I could imagine to my home on the same night for a round-table discussion that later wound up being the basis of a radio program that I did. (I had a talk show on the radio.) It became clear to me that there was not a religious construction on this earth within which I felt comfortable—this sounds almost spiritually arrogant, and I truly don't mean it to be so, but for one reason or another, there was always something in a particular paradigm, whatever it was, that I had to move back from.

I think probably a lot of people share that experience.

No matter where I looked, and I looked into Far Eastern religions, I looked at everything. Every time I would begin to feel mildly comfortable, I would run across a piece of dogma or a certain particular construction that pushed me away, and I would say, "No, no, no, this can't be it. This doesn't feel right to me." Not unlike Joseph Smith's wonderful story, who founded the Mormon church, I could not find a church that made sense to me.

Neither did he, and so, according to Mormon theology, he asked God one day out in a field which church is the one true church. God appeared to him and said, "There isn't any." Then Joseph Smith made what I think was a big mistake. He created a church and said that *it* was the One True Church. *More* dogma.

Going back to the depression you were in, did you just start writing and suddenly realize you're having a conversation with God? How did that happen?

It was something like that. I woke up on this particular day in February of 1992 at four o'clock in the morning. I was very, very upset. I threw back the covers and marched out of the bedroom. I didn't know where I was going. I was just marching down the hall, going nowhere. The house was dark; it's four o'clock in the morning. I was angry. I was upset. I woke up in a fit of frustration, not having any idea what was going on. I thought, Well, my answer is where I have found answers before—but there was nothing in the refrigerator of interest to me. I closed the refrigerator door and went to the living room and sat there in the dark. Only someone who has been chronically depressed can understand this. I sat in the living room, in the dark, at four o'clock in the morning doing nothing but looking at the darkness and the four walls. Stewing in my own juice, as it were.

Somewhere in the next few moments, my eyes glanced down and I saw a yellow legal pad on the coffee table. I reached down, picked it up, and a pen that was nearby. I thought, Well, I'll get some of this anger out. I began writing a very angry letter to no one in particular. The letter was addressed to no one. I just started off in the middle of a thought. I was so emotional. What is going here? Why can't I make this work? It was a very angry letter, with each sentence punctuated by four or five exclamation points and sixteen question marks. What do I have to do? What do I have to know? Somebody tell me the rules. It was one of those times when you cry out in the middle of the night to the universe for some kind of answer.

I sat there with a little light on next to the couch and started writing that letter. I wrote and wrote and wrote my heart out with anger and frustration for about 20 minutes. You know how when you're really angry sometimes, you write very large. I must have filled up six sheets with one sentence each, just huge, huge letters scribbled across the page, across the tablet. Finally, I was done with my unanswerable questions. I was feeling a bit becalmed. It was a mildly therapeutic adventure. I was about to put the pen down when it felt in my mind as if there was something more I wanted to say—a postscript, or something. I brought the pen back to the tablet, and the first thought that came to my mind I wrote down. The thought was: *Do you really want answers to all of these questions, or are you just venting?* I had the impression that the thought was coming from another source. I looked at that question on the tablet and laughed a bit at it, and I thought, Well, I'll have some fun with my mind here, and I answered my own question. *Yes, I'm venting, but if you have answers, I'd sure as hell like to have them.*

The next thought that came to my mind I also wrote down, which was: *You* are *sure as hell, but wouldn't it be nice to be sure as heaven?* I thought then, Gee, what's going on here? My mood had changed, I noticed that. I was feeling a little bit lighter, and so I thought, Well, I'll continue. Maybe I'm having a wonderful game with my mind. That's exactly what I thought I was doing, just playing with my mind. I know this sounds a little bit strange, but I started writing back and forth to myself, and before I knew it I was engaged in a fascinating dialogue that went on for about two-and-a-half hours, until it was 7:15 in the morning. At no time did I go back over the pages. I just kept on writing and moving ahead, moving ahead in this dialogue until, somewhere around a quarter after seven in the morning, I put the pen down, and then and only then did I start flipping the pages of this yellow legal pad back to see what I had written. When I began reading what I had written, I realized I had something very, very unusual.

Did you have a sense that you could go back to it and you wouldn't lose it?

No, I did not have that sense. I never had any idea that it would go on beyond that morning. It was just a series of questions and answers that I found fascinating, and I looked at the answers, and I thought, Hmm, because some of the answers, I thought, were profound. So I enjoyed the exchange, and at that point I went to bed, actually, because I'd been up since the middle of the night. It was a Saturday morning, as I recall. I didn't have to go to work that day, and I went back to bed, and that was the end of that, except that the next morning at precisely quarter after four in the morning, I was awakened with an urge to return to that yellow legal pad. It was a great hunger, is the only way I could describe it. I woke up in the middle of the night with a knowingness that I needed to get back to that piece of paper. So I did. I didn't question it. I threw back the covers, and this time not with anger, but with great anticipation.

I danced out of the bedroom and found that legal pad and began writing some more. That went on for three weeks, almost always between four and five in the morning. I continued to ask questions and get answers and have a running dialogue—not just questions and answers, but comments back and forth just as if I was talking to someone. Like we're talking here, only on paper. Again, I found it very fascinating. My mood was lifting rapidly, and I was beginning to see life and things differently even in just that first short three-week period. Although the dialogue did continue on and off for the next year, I didn't tell many people about it. In fact, only two other people in my whole life knew about it. It was a very private experience.

It sounds to me that what was going on was something that was outside of your thinking mind, your intellect. That you were just putting the words on paper and not really thinking about them. Is that what was happening?

That's exactly what was happening. It was like taking dictation. I would look at what was coming off the pen and onto the tablet, and I would read it as it was being written. As I would read it, of course, I would have a response. I'd have a reaction to it, and I would write down my reaction. Maybe my reaction was, What does that mean? Or maybe my reaction was, I can't believe that, whatever it was. Or maybe my reaction was the next logical question in a dialogue. Almost immediately after I would finish writing, another thought would enter my mind as if someone had simply placed it there, or maybe was whispering into my right ear. A voiceless voice, if you will, that was simply putting that next thought there. As soon as the thought arrived in my mind—and sometimes it wasn't even a complete sentence when it began—I would begin to write. I would write as fast as I could and still hold the thought.

Once or twice, I have to say, it got kind of comical because the thoughts would come so rapidly that once I recall saying to no one—mind you, it's four o'clock in the morning and there's no one in the room—"Not so fast. Not so fast." I can recall saying that out loud, you know. Then I looked around the room and thought, Oh, if someone catches me here, I'm really going to go to the looney bin. But no sooner did I say "not so fast," then, in fact, the flow of those thoughts slowed down! So that I could get it all down in handwriting. The entire dialogue was handwritten.

When did you have—or did you have a sense at some point— that you were actually engaged in writing a book? Something that would be published?

I didn't have a sense that I was writing a book that would be published. Even though it did say to me, the voiceless voice did say to me, "This will be a book"—relatively early in the experience. But I thought, Yeah, right, of course. You know, everyone in the world is writing a book these days, and certainly my little mind game with myself is going to be a book that someone's going to publish. I didn't really hold a high level of belief about that. I always thought it would be a private experience that I was having with my own mind. One's writing in one's own journal. I considered it that till the very end. A very private writing in my private journal. I never imagined that we would be sitting here talking on a national radio program, or that I would be seeing people from Toronto to Miami who had read the book and were discussing it with me. That was the furthest thing from my mind. So I did not have a sense of "I'm writing a book here." I had a sense of "I'm having a marvelous experience in my journal, in my private journal."

What led from this just being a private, personal, intimate journal that you were writing in to becoming a book? What was that process?

In at least two places in the dialogue, I was told point blank that it would be a book one day. As I said, even though I didn't believe that, I heard it. I began to think, when it was finished, I wonder if this *is* supposed to be a book? So I showed the manuscript, the handwritten manuscript, to one or two close friends, people very close to me. Both of those people looked at me wide-eyed after reading just 20 or 30 pages and said, "You *are* going to get this published, aren't you?" I said no. I mean, I hadn't thought about it. Do you think I should? Both people, independent of each other—this was at two different times—said to me, "Neale, if you don't at least send this to a publisher, you've got to be crazy. This is marvelous stuff. This is incredible stuff."

So with that encouragement, I thought, Well, I'll at least get it typed, because it was all handwritten. I had about 550 handwritten yellow legal pad pages. So I thought, Well, I'll at least go that far. Then I'll see how it looks when I read it back. Sometimes when I read things myself in typeset form, I have a different feeling about them. I'll see how it looks once it's typeset. I sent it off to a professional typesetter who took a year to typeset it because I didn't have any money. This lady didn't know me. She was a stranger. But she said, "Well, if you'll give me like a hundred dollars a month on a retainer, I'll squeeze it in between my other projects whenever I can." It took her a year to do it. I said to her during that year, "I don't want to see this material. Don't send it to me. Don't show it to me. I don't want any comments on it. Just do it." She did. She would call me every so often to let me know how she was doing with it, but never made any comment about the material. A year later she called and told me it was finished. She had kind of a teary voice. I said, "Well, I'll come by and pick it up." She said, "I need you to know this is the most astonishing material I've ever typed for anyone. Where did you get this?"

This is not a New Age person. This is a typesetter, for heaven's sake, in the business of setting people's type. I thought, Wow! What an interesting reaction from somebody who is so far removed from my circle of friends and from my area of influence. She was so taken with the material that she insisted that I send it to a publisher. In fact, what she said was, "If you don't, I will." So I did.

So did the first publisher who got it take it?

No, the first four rejected it, actually. The fifth publisher to whom I sent it did, in fact, reject it as well. But they rejected it in a way that was a mistake. They sent me a form letter that was one of four form letters that they send out to people. But the secretary made a mistake and sent the wrong form letter to me. I've since heard the details of this story. Because I got the wrong form letter, I immediately knew that they hadn't read the book. The form letter they sent me was a form letter they send to people whose material did not match what they were publishing. It said, *Please look for a publisher who publishes material more along the lines of what's in your manuscript.* I knew, of course, that my manuscript perfectly suited their titles list. So I said to myself, "Those rascals never even cracked the cover!"

Well, they had, in fact, scanned the book, but the secretary sent me letter B instead of letter A. But that generated a little anger inside of me, and so that happy mistake caused me to resubmit it. I sent a letter back to the chief editor of that company and I said, "Please don't insult me by rejecting my book without even reading it. If you read it and say you don't like it, I'll understand, but you must at least read it before I'll accept your rejection as final." I shot the letter right back the same day I got his letter of rejection. In addition, I called the company. I asked if I could have the name of the owner of the place, and I shot another copy of my manuscript to him with a handwritten note inside, not even a typed, written letter. Just a quick note that I wrote, and it said, "Read any ten pages." That's all it said. He, in fact, is the one who chose to publish the book. The publisher read the book on a challenge, on a dare, because I put a note in there: "Read any ten pages." A very unorthodox way to approach a publisher. He did flip through it and picked out ten pages at random. Not long after, he picked up the phone and called me and said, "We want to do this book."

How has the book changed your life?

I think the most profound change in my life is the surety, if that's a word, with which I approach the subject of God. I used to think that God was real. I used to think that God was responsive to the human condition, to our circumstance here. I used to think that God would answer prayers. I used to think that God loved us, without condition. I used to think all those things. Now I don't anymore. Now I *know* them. I've moved into a place of absolute knowing about those things. So the biggest change in my life, and at the same time the most beneficial, has been a huge shift in my place of beingness with regard to the experience of God. I'm no longer in this place of wondering or even thinking or even believing. I moved from believing in God to knowing God as a very good friend, a good friend to have. That, in turn, has produced other much smaller and less significant, but nevertheless noteworthy, changes in my life as well. My relationships have all improved dramatically. My financial life is beyond my wildest dreams. My health—I feel better now than I did ten years ago, probably look better, too.

As you encounter people who have read the book, what are some of the more important things that people have gravitated toward that are in the book?

I think three messages that people really get out of the book that are important to them is, number one, God is wonderful. That God is not going to get you. God is not going to punish us. That God loves us truly unconditionally. God is wonderful, with a great sense of humor. To put it in one sentence, that *God is on our side.* That, more than anything else, is what I hear now in the mail that we receive, and we're getting over a thousand letters a month from people from all over the world. Every letter, almost without exception, begins with that. "Thank you, Neale. Thank you. Thank you. Thank you for bringing me to an even greater clarity about who and what God really is. That God is our friend. That God's not going to get us. That God is not this demon in the skies who lives in the space of judgment and in great wrath. That God is not a jealous God," and all those things.

The second most important thing that people get out of the book is how crazy we are in the way that we think. That most of our thoughts about most things are what I want to loosely call "wrong thoughts." That by thinking wrongly, we are creating a life for ourselves, individually and collectively on the planet, which in no way reflects out highest goals or desires, but in fact has created a trap from which, it appears on the surface, we have no way of extricating ourselves. So I think that most people read the book, and they kind of hit their forehead with the palm of their hand like, "Duh! Oh, I get it!" I think that the book makes it more clear. Many other New Thought and New Age books have made this point, but I'm not sure that any have made it quite as vividly and quite as expressively as this one. That truly, as you believe, so will it be done unto you. This book has caused people to change the whole way they hold their life, and the whole way they think about things.

The third and last thing that I hear people telling me they got out of the book was that we had to learn how to communicate back to God. We had to learn how to pray, if you will, differently. We had to learn how to open the channel of communication both ways. When we do that, we will have formed an effective and wonderful relationship with God—the likes of which most people on this planet rarely ever conceive of, much less experience. So people are now forming study groups spontaneously all over the world.

I had a person in Seattle tell me the other day—and in almost every city I go to—we're forming a study group. We are getting letters from Australia, Germany, from France, we're forming a study group. Study groups are forming around the material of this book all over the world. It apparently is saying something to people that's real common, that's very important to all of us. I think it speaks to people at a soul level, which I think is exactly what God intended when He dictated the book to me.

Everyone wants to know what prayer is really about. Would you perhaps give us a little insight into that?

The startling statement is that prayer is not necessary. I mean prayer in the way most people have been praying. Most people say prayers of supplication. That is, we turn to God when there is something we want or need, as a rule. We pray, Please help me get better, or let me have this new job, or don't get me fired, or let me heal from this disease, or help Grandma Jane get over her cancer—whatever it is we're trying to pray for. Our prayers are prayers of supplication, and what God said in this book is, "Come to Me in any way you want." There's not a right and a wrong way to do this, but there are some ways that are somewhat more effective than other ways. God said to me that praying prayers of supplication will not be nearly as effective as praying prayers of thanks. I asked, "Well, you know, how can I be grateful or thankful for something that is not in my experience?" God said, "Even before you ask, I will have answered." The secret of the universe is that all things have already happened. See, we're living in a timeless timeline where all effects have already taken place. When we experience that we are in this place called time/no time/now/always—in the eternal moment of now—that is what God was trying to help me understand.

What God has been explaining to me very patiently through these books is that we are living in an eternal moment of always. Time is not a left-to-right configuration. Before, now, and after is an absolute figment of our imagination. Because all things that have ever happened and ever will happen are happening in this moment now. That is not just a concept; it is literally true. So that even before you ask, He will have answered. By the way, I might even add that all possible outcomes of every single circumstance have already occurred.

Sounds something like Heisenberg's uncertainty principle.

Isn't that interesting. It's a fascinating concept. The point I was trying to make in the first book was simply that every master in the world has known this. I don't care what religious or spiritual tradition you look at, every master has gone to God with a prayer of gratitude, never with a prayer of supplication. Never asking like Roger Rabbit: *Please!* But rather, going to God saying, *Thank you, God, for this experience that has already occurred.*

For what I already have.

Yes, for what I already have. *A Course in Miracles,* I thought, put it beautifully: "Thank you, God, for helping me understand that this problem has already been solved for me." Remarkable statement.

When you go to God in supplication, you are saying, "I want this." That's basing prayer on wanting and not having.

It was explained to me very clearly that the universe will provide to you exactly what you declare. Therefore, if you declare, "Oh God, I wish I could have more money. I want, want, want more money." God will say, "Okay, fine, I'll give you the experience of wanting more money." God is a great Xerox machine in the sky, duplicating your thoughts and putting them into form in your life in the very next instant. Therefore, out of the words of your own mouth will you condemn yourself. So if your prayer is, I want more money; God, can't you hear me? I want more money! Then God will give you that experience. This whole theory can be reduced to one sentence: God always says yes. God does not say no. So God says yes to everything you think, say, and do. If you're thinking, saying, and acting out "I want more money," you, in fact, will have the experience of wanting more money. So what God invites us to notice is that the correct prayer is a prayer of thanks and supplication, in that we already have it. The engine that drives the human experience of creation are the words *I* and *I am*. Whatever you say following the word *I am,* if you say it often enough and with enough conviction, will, in fact, become your reality.

I recall that quote when Jesus said that I and the father are one. From what you're saying, he meant it.

I believe Jesus meant it literally. In fact, more of what Jesus had to say was meant literally than we would think. If we begin to take the words of Jesus—except, of course, for the obvious parables—as quite literal, we suddenly get to the true metaphysical meaning in the Bible. "I and my father are one" is another one. Of course, "Have I not said ye are Gods?" A third extraordinary statement that he meant quite literally was "These things and more shall you do, also. Why are you so amazed?"

I guess it's part of the entrainment that every one of us raised in Western culture has. We think that somehow God is something far greater than any of us can imagine, particularly those of us who may have been raised Catholic. We had many intervenors between us and God, not the least of which were Jesus, Mary, and all the saints. Even becoming a saint was really outside of merely being human. It's easy to understand why a lot of people would have trouble imagining themselves as one with the Creator. In fact, Jesus got crucified for saying it.

Yes, he did. On the other hand, it was written that he allowed himself to be. The crucifixion of Jesus was not something that occurred against his will.

It certainly puts a new light on Judas, doesn't it?

Yes, of course. All things happen perfectly. Jesus would have said, "Well, do you think that this happened against my will? Do you not know that I could call upon legions of angels and stop this thing right now?"

One of the things that's interesting to me is a concept presented in your book—when God talks about immortality—that the body was designed to live forever. That's pretty wild.

Yes, it is. Yet there are people, it's been said—I don't know how true it is—but I've read some books about it, that many hundreds of years ago, people lived to be far older than we do today, interestingly enough.

In the Bible, in the Old Testament, particularly, there are individuals who lived for eight or nine hundred years. Maybe that wasn't just an illusory myth.

I think that biophysically when you look at the human body, there's really no reason why it should wear out. I mean, no reason in nature. The reasons that the body wears out, and certainly the reason it wears out as fast as it does, have to do with how we treat it, the way we treat ourselves. Most people treat their cars better than they treat their bodies.

When I was ten years old, I saw a parrot in the Washington zoo that was alive when George Washington was alive. Parrots live a long time. Some animals don't live a long time. But others, like tortoises, can live hundreds of years. I thought to myself, Why do parrots live longer than human beings?

Surely the human being was designed to be at least as magnificent as your nearest tortoise, one would hope. In fact, originally, it was true. The tortoise isn't making nearly as many bad choices, however, as we are. Some animals, most animals, aren't making choices consciously. I mean, they're not looking at this and saying, "I shouldn't eat this, it's bad for me." We, on the other hand, are saying, "I shouldn't eat that; it's bad for me," and eating it anyway.

Going back to some of the insights that are in the book, this is a quote: "The deepest secret is that life is not a process of discovery, but a process of creation."

We're all running around trying to learn. For years, I was thinking, Gee, if I only knew the secret. Whatever the secret is. How to make relationships work. How to make life work at every level. If I only knew. So I had this idea that if I turned over enough rocks or looked behind enough trees or listened to enough sermons or bought enough tapes, I would finally understand it, and I would awaken to a brand new level of awareness. I went on a year-long binge of learning, learning—trying to learn all I could learn. What God said to me in this book was, Hey, you have nothing to learn. You never did have anything to learn. You have only to remember what you have always known.

No one needs to tell a baby about love, or about joy, or about not lying, about truth or honesty. You know, babies are honest. One-year-olds are honest. Lying is a learned reaction, as is just about everything else. If only all of us could go through our lives simply demonstrating what we already know about love, compassion, honesty, truthfulness, about life itself, rather than trying to learn something that we imagine we don't know. Stop the search and act right now as if you knew the grandest truths of the universe, because you do. No one has to teach you what's the most loving thing to do in any particular situation. A five-word sentence would change the world tomorrow if, at every single choice-point in our collective lives, we simply stopped and asked ourselves the question: "What would love do now? What would love do now? Okay, good. Now what would love do?" Thank you very much, and *now* what would love do? If we'll ask ourselves that question with earnestness and with purity of heart, the answer will be immediately apparent to us, and we will discover that we do not have to learn anything. We merely have to live a life that demonstrates that we already know those answers.

People who come from that place are called masters. We imagine that they've learned all this great stuff. No, they haven't learned a damned thing. See, we've learned lots of damned things in our life. We need to forget all those damned things we've learned and start acting as if we always knew the highest truth, because we do.

So we need to forget the devil's advocate and go after heaven's advocate?

Yes, go after heaven's advocate.

The concept of "You create your own reality," runs through at least the first volume of Conversations with God. *This is a concept, an idea, that has been around for a few decades now. This idea that you create your own reality. There's a lot of misunderstanding about it.*

For a few centuries. I think there was a master who walked the planet who once said, "As you believe, so will it be done unto you."

I believe that saying has been abused in the area of health. People say, "So you have cancer. Well, how did you create that?" Or, "What did you do to create this in your life?" Can you share your insights on this idea of creating your own reality with regard to illness?

That question is the most irrelevant question. Apart from the fact that it's a very heartless question, it's also a pointless one. The important question is not, Why did you give yourself that situation, condition, or circumstance, but what do you choose now? *Why* is the most irrelevant question in the human experience. Clearly, if we knew why we were choosing something as dreadful as cancer, for instance, we wouldn't have chosen it. If we were simply doing that mechanistically, we would never do it. No one walks into a wall deliberately. That's kind of a dumb question. You think I did it on purpose? If I knew why, I wouldn't have done it! So the question is irrelevant.

The only really important thing to know is that you are being the creator of your own experience. Notice the circumstances and situations with which you have surrounded yourself. If you are able to accept full responsibility for those circumstances without needing to know why you did that, then in that moment you're able to change the circumstance or move toward accepting the possibility that such changes *are*, in fact, *possible*. But if you are positioning yourself as a victim of the universe—no, no, no, I didn't have anything to do with this, Neale, you don't understand. I don't create my own reality. I didn't bring this cancer on. I didn't bring this job loss on. I did not create the end of this relationship. I'm simply a victim of circumstances here. Then, of course, you're powerless from that moment on to change anything, because you'll forever position yourself as a person who's at the effect of the entire universe, which, of course, is not true.

Even if you don't agree that you are the creator of your own universe, you could at least move to a place where you say, Well, with God on my side, I can create anything I want. If God will help me, I can do anything. That's a more traditional point of view about things. It's not altogether an unhealthy point of view.

People who have an extraordinary faith in God, whether or not they believe they're creating their own reality, find that they have enormous strength to recreate the circumstances of their life by calling on God to do so. Only after they do that about fifty or a hundred times do they realize that they've *always* had that power, and that God's given that ability to everyone.

There's one more quote that I want to have you comment on: "To live your life without expectation, without the need for specific results, that is freedom, that is Godliness, that is how I live." This is God speaking, of course. Is this living in the moment? Does it mean giving up control?

Yes, it means giving up the need for any particular result. To the degree that we're attached to any particular result, to that degree we are dependent upon it for the experience called happiness. True masters understand that the way out of that dilemma and that trap is to have no particular need for any given result. That, of course, leads to larger questions, like: If we're not to have any particular results that we can expect or want or need, then what is the point of life?

Many of the answers to the questions we've been discussing also raise more good questions.

As all good answers should. I'm always suspicious of an answer that leaves no questions in its wake. Every *good* answer leaves a question in its wake. That's the measure that I use as to whether it's a good answer or not.

Is there anything else you'd like to share with our readers?

I'm not real special in this regard, with respect to the conversation I had with God. I think that the largest message I would like to share is that everyone may have a conversation with God. In fact, everyone is, all the time. I hope that people will be more in touch with their own process of communicating with God, and use the process fruitfully and wonderfully for the rest of their lives.

EPILOGUE

If there's only one message you take away from Neale Donald Walsch's talks with God, it's that God/dess or whatever term or idea fits your version of the All That Is, is, indeed, on our side. The cosmos is not an unfriendly black hole, and we can communicate with the God force. He/She/It is there for us if only we can reach out and make the connection, simply by being open and receptive.

Another provocative insight Walsch reveals through his dialogue with God is that we already have whatever we think we need or want, "Even before you ask, He will have answered." Walsch brings the Divine into the personal realm, like talking with an old and trusted friend whose love is beyond question. Prayer takes the form of a spirited conversation between the self and the Super Self. We are all having a conversation with God all the time, according to Walsch. The key is learning how to listen.

CHAPTER TEN

THE ONENESS IN ALL

Father Bede Griffiths, with Michael Toms

PROLOGUE

*T*he late mythologist Joseph Campbell once suggested that the
new mythology would be a planetary one encompassing the
entire earth and its inhabitants. Clearly, we belong to one world,
and a new planet-wide myth will necessarily embrace the spirit
connecting all life. This can only happen as each of us recognizes
our face in the other, as we're able to come to a deeper understanding of the mysterious thread that ties us to everything and
everyone else. The importance of such a task cannot be underes-
timated in a world so clearly dependent on the active cooperation
of all of its residents. We have to get beyond our differences and
embrace the oneness we all share at the deepest level.

There are a few pointriders, spiritual pioneers, as it were,
among us, who have dedicated their lives to recovering this lost

heritage of humankind. One of them has been Father Bede Griffiths, a Benedictine monk who lived in India for nearly 40 years. In 1955 he founded a Christian-Hindu ashram in south India in order to live according to monastic precepts and further the reunion of the world's great religions. He authored Vedanta and Christian Faith, Marriage of East and West, The Golden String, The Cosmic Revelation, *and other books.*

MICHAEL TOMS: *Before you went to India, you studied at Oxford, and one of your tutors was C. S. Lewis. I found that fascinating. Could you tell us about your relationship with C. S. Lewis?*

FATHER BEDE GRIFFITHS: Yes, it was very interesting because, when I first met him—it must have been in 1927—he had just joined Magdalen College as a tutor, and I came as an undergraduate, and neither of us were Christians at that time. We both had a Christian background, but we'd moved out of it, and we were both searching, in a very general way. And it was really two years before we shared with one another, and we began to discover Christianity together. It was an extraordinary experience. We met from time to time, we corresponded, and within about two years, each of us came to a very strong Christian conviction. But of course we also remained open in other ways as we'd been accustomed for so long.

You were also influenced by the writings of D. H. Lawrence, then, weren't you?

Yes. That was my earlier stage. You see, I was worried about being overly intellectual, a whole education of school and Oxford with this very intellectual study—I did Latin and Greek and so on—and I felt I was in a prison. And D. H. Lawrence was one of those who opened the prison doors for me—opened me to nature, to humanity, you could say, in a sense, and to the whole sensual dimensions of nature. Because we tend to live in the mind and neglect the body. I think Lawrence was one of the prophets who wanted to reinstate the body and its values in human life.

And he also opened you to the unconscious realm, as well.

He opened the unconscious, but mostly that came more through Jung.

I met a very wonderful Jungian analyst, Toni Sussman. She was one of Jung's first disciples, actually, and opened all of these dimensions of the unconscious for me. Since then Jung has been a great influence in my life, really, and I can't think now except in terms of the unconscious—not limited to Jung's fuel, perhaps going beyond it in some way, but still very definitely based on his understanding.

You became a member of a Benedictine abbey there in England for a while, and then, what was the bridge that took you to India?

Well, now, Toni Sussman was a bridge in some way. You see, she not only opened me up to the unconscious, but also to Oriental mysticism. I knew very little—it was 1940. She had all of these books, and she had a center for meditation in London. We became great friends. That was my opening to India, really. For the next few years I was reading about Vedanta and yoga, and the desire to go to India was there.

Then in 1948, I think it must have been, an Indian Benedictine monk came to my monastery in England and asked whether I would come with him to start a foundation in India. So in 1955, we received permission to come together and start it outside Bangalore in India.

It is in south India. Bangalore is perhaps the most prosperous city in south India.

This is Satchitananda Ashram. Satchitananda—it's the name of the godhead in Hinduism: *Sat* is being; *chit* is knowledge, wisdom; and *ananda* is bliss. And we take it as a symbol of the Trinity—being, wisdom, and love—so that is the name for our ashram.

I think those of us, particularly those who live in the United States, have images that we conjure up when we hear the word ashram *or* monastery. *We see walls and buildings. Can you describe your ashram or monastery at Satchitananda.*

Well, in a sense, the ashram's the opposite of a monastery. A monastery does have walls and buildings, but an ashram in the Indian tradition is a group of disciples gathered around a master, and normally they have little huts. In our ashram, we each have a little thatched hut. We live together among the trees, meet together for prayer and for meals, and for sharing, but it's an open community. A monastery tends to have an enclosure—keeps people out. An ashram is always an open community—we're open to everybody. People come from all over the world now. And also, what is important is the village people. They can come equally freely, so we aim at being, really, an open community, open to the world and open to the spiritual values wherever they are to be found.

Can you describe a typical day at the Satchitananda ashram?

Yes. We get up at five o'clock, which is rather late in India; many would get up at four. When I first came, we got up at three o'clock. But five is a reasonable hour. Then we always have an hour for meditation beside the river Khavery—it's called "The Ganges of the South"—it's nearly a mile across, a beautiful river. Most people go and meditate by the river at sunrise. And that is very important, to recollect oneself, let things go, simply be in the presence of God and the nature around you. That is the beginning of the day. Then we meet for prayer. And our prayer is very interesting; it's grown over the years. We always begin with Sanskrit chanting. You see, Sanskrit's the most ancient language of India, and really, in a sense, the foundation of Indian culture. We always chant the Gayatri mantra, the most sacred mantra in the Vedas, and then we do some other prayers from the Vedas. Then we often read from different scriptures—Hindu, Buddhist, Taoist, Sikh, and so on. And then we read from the Bible and have a psalm or some other Christian prayer. We try to integrate these different traditions in our daily prayer. It's centered on Christ; we are Christian people, a Christian community, but we open it to the values of the other traditions.

So in many ways, the Satchitananda ashram that you maintain in India is ecumenical.

It's really ecumenical. The value of meditation is that you don't have to have a God or any particular form. You sit and calm your body, your mind, and your senses, and then when you reach the state of calm, you get beyond the senses and the mind with all of its rational concepts, and you become aware of your inner self. They call it *atmanvidya* or experience of the self. Many people come to the ashram from different parts of America, and all are seeking this deeper center, to find the real meaning of their lives. You're caught up in the world of outer things all the time, and worse still, perhaps, of concepts and rational ideas and science, and so on. To get beyond all that and discover your innermost being or real self—that is what people seek. Our ashram really is open to anybody who is seeking to find themselves: "Who am I?" is what we ask. And for a Christian, you find yourself in Christ, but others find another way.

Many of us who are used to observing Christian institutions in this country would call that a rather advanced concept for a Christian institution. How has the established Church related to what you're doing?

Well, on the whole we've been very fortunate, because Christians can be, and Roman Catholics, particularly, extremely narrow, and really reject almost any other religion. But the Vatican Council II made an immense difference in the Catholic church. It really opened itself. There's a wonderful saying: It said, "The Church rejects nothing that is true and holy in other religions, and Catholics should recognize, preserve, and promote the spiritual and moral values of other religions." So that is our basis. As a result, most of the leaders of the Church in India have supported us, and also in Rome. We belong to the Camaldolese congregation, which is in Italy, and they have a base in Rome, so that we've really had a very good acceptance. Now people come to our ashram from religious orders in India—the Jesuits, Franciscans, and others—and they see in us an authentically Christian ashram. And I think that's important.

Father Bede, in the Middle East we have three of the major religious traditions fighting one another tooth and nail. What about that? How are we going to solve this dilemma?

I see that as a great problem, and it's what I'm most interested in. In our ashram, we've gotten in the habit now of reading from the different Scriptures. And day to day you learn to relate them. I'm preparing a book now, actually, of readings from the Scriptures of the world. I want people to be able to meditate on the different Scriptures in the light of their own traditions. You don't have to leave your tradition, but you must learn to listen to the revelations of another tradition. So this meeting of religions is, for me, the great need.

The theme I've put forward is that every religion begins with a certain dualism—you have God and the world, and so on—but in each religion the movement is towards *non*-duality. Not monism, not one, and not two. Non-duality goes beyond the one and the two. It's very clear in Hinduism and Buddhism. Islam,

Judaism, and Christianity are a problem; they are very dualistic: God and the world are separate; God and humanity are separate; good and evil are separate, and heaven and hell are separate.

But I believe that this kind of dualism is a stage we have to go through. You have to make these distinctions, and then you have to go beyond them. And this occurs in every tradition. In Islam, you have the Sufis, who go right beyond the dualism. In Judaism you have the Kabbalah, which is a mystical tradition. So the mystical tradition in each religion transcends the dualism and discovers the one reality that is not one and not two; it's a mystery beyond human reason. That is the point. Your reason cannot grasp it. You've got to allow it to reveal itself to you.

Hinduism and Buddhism are opposites, in a sense, but at heart they're one.

Speaking of other traditions, both Buddhism and Hinduism took birth in India.

Yes, exactly. We have really found opposites. The Buddha rejected the Vedic tradition—the sacrifice, the priesthood, caste, all these things—and freed himself. But the depth of his insight was really one with the insight of the Upanishads and the Hindu tradition. That's my belief, that behind the differences in religion— they're cultural, largely, the ritual, the doctrine and the organization—there is a hidden mystery. That mystery is present, under a different form, in each religion. And we have to distinguish between the limited form, which is historical or cultural, and the hidden mystery, which is absolute in each tradition, beyond word and beyond thought, you see. That is the center of all religion.

I know you've been interested in the areas of science and religion coming together, and what you were saying made me think of the physicist David Bohm talking about the implicate order and the explicate order, and how it's all implicit.

Yes, David Bohm is a friend of Krishnamurti. Apparently he's a first-class scientist; he's fully respected. He was a friend of Einstein. On that ground he's perfectly sound. At the same time, he knows meditation, and he's been able to go beyond the limits of science and recognize what he calls the implicate order. Everything is enfolded—the whole world of nature, of humanity, is all an unfolding. But behind all of these explications, there's something implicit. Behind it all, behind the whole universe, behind all humanity, there is this hidden presence, and that is one. The One is behind the many. Bohm is the leading scientist who has opened the way to seeing science, with all its study of the multiple orders of creation, and how we can relate that to the inner center where everything is implicit.

The Hindu search is to find that inner center where the whole universe is in you. They say there's a little shrine in the heart, and that space is the whole universe. So the universe is outside you— we project it outside ourselves—but at the same time the universe is inside. When you die, you leave the outer universe, but you enter the inner universe; you become one with the whole. That is the end, you see.

In the Resurrection, literally and actually, the body of Jesus was taken down from the cross and put in the grave and was transformed into subtle body. That transformation can take place because it's a gross body manifesting in the outer world, but there's a subtle body that can manifest but also can disappear— Jesus appears and disappears. At the ascension, that subtle body was taken into the spiritual body, to the eternal, and is no longer in space or in time. For me, resurrection is the passage of nature, creation, matter, life, and humanity into the spaceless, timeless, eternal reality, to the implicate order beyond all outer form, to the resurrection—one with the One.

Tibetans have the tradition of the rainbow body, which is similar.

Very similar, yes. It's in many traditions. It's in the Chinese; the Taoists call it the "diamond body," and there's a wonderful saint in south India who is supposed to have had this golden body. They say nobody could take a photo of him [laughs]. I don't know whether it's true.

The story is—you can believe it or not—that as the end came, he asked his disciples to build him a little hut. He entered into the hut and they locked the door. He told them to come back after three days. And after three days they returned, and nothing was there.

You must understand that gross matter is a form of matter. Behind the gross matter there is subtle matter. Science is beginning to recognize this subtle matter. It has an effect on gross matter, but you can't see it and you can't measure it. And beyond the subtle matter is the inner, implicit, implicate order, which is the reality. The one reality manifests, in the subtle world and in the gross world, and the aim of humanity is to go through the gross to the subtle, and then to the final fullness of the one reality. That is our goal.

When I was a child in school, the idea of being a saint was totally beyond any of us, but was held out as a goal to achieve. What I hear you saying, and what has come out from a number of other contemplatives and thinkers in the last few years—the most profound understanding that's emerged in the last decade or two, particularly in Christianity—is the idea that one can experience God, the spirit, in this life, all the time.

Yes, it's this problem of body, soul, and spirit. Unfortunately, in the Church the idea grew up that you have to become holy spiritually. Many Christians simply neglect the body; the body is simply of this world. They even neglect the psyche. They leave all that, and think that by the spirit alone they will be united with God.

But you're human! You cannot be united with God, with the

spirit, unless your mind and your body are integrated. Today we're discovering it's through the body and the mind, integrated in the spirit, that we become holy. Many very simple people, living much more normal, natural lives, are at a deeper spiritual level than many monks and religious people. There are stories of the fathers in the desert who would say, "Who is the most holy man of all?" And they would say, "Some man in Alexandria, deep in the garden—he's the really holy man." So we're discovering that this holiness is open to every human being, really, and holiness is wholeness, to become whole. It's the same word, you know—*wholeness, holiness,* and *health* are all the same root, so that the body, mind, and spirit have all to be integrated in the whole.

I think one of the criticisms—and it probably emerges from the Marxist idea of material reality—is that somehow pursuing religion, pursuing the spirit, being of the spirit, excludes being involved in social problems, solving the social ills of the world. What about this?

Well, that's the same problem, really. The Church generally concentrated on the life of the spirit, which is of course the most important, in its way—but it meant they neglected the social dimension. To be a saint was to be holy in your individual, personal life. You had no necessary connection to the social order, to politics, or anything like that. And there again, today, we're seeing, as Aristotle said, political animals—we belong to a human society, and you can't actually become whole as a human being unless you relate to the society in which you live and all the problems of it. So now we have this invention of liberation theology. The Areopagite, whom most people today think was a Syrian monk of the sixth century—he brought this out into full light. It's really trying to integrate the economic and the social order into this order of holiness. It's not outside; it's part of it. But again, it's difficult to bring those together.

The tradition of the Church is very individualistic. The saints are these holy people, as you said, much beyond all ordinary human beings, and you're trying to become a saint like that. And so the political, social, economic order is put down. Of course, the Church today tries to recognize it and do something of meaning towards it, but it's not seen as part of sanctity. I think liberation theologians are discovering that simple people in South America and Brazil, particularly, simple peasant people, discover this. They find it through their social relationship, their concern for one another, and they reach a degree of holiness. They are finding God in their social and even their political and economic conditions, is the thing.

This brings to mind the question of the darkness, the problems of the world, and having to experience one's own inner darkness in order to really wrestle with what we see outside, which is really inside. There's a notion that somehow we have to always go for the light; yet you've written about Dionysus and the Divine darkness. I think that's useful because there needs to be a balance between the light and the dark.

Yes. It's part of the same problem, concentrating on the mind and the spirit and neglecting the body, the senses, the emotions, the dark side of our nature. And actually God is just as much in the dark as in the light. Actually, it was Gregory of Nyssa who was the real founder of Christian mysticism—he had the three ways: the way of the purgative way, freeing yourself from sin, attachment to the world; then the illuminative way, opening to the revelation of God and creation, humanity, incarnation, and so on; then the unitive way, finding God in the darkness—beyond all word and thought you encounter the hidden mystery. And that's beyond your mind and all its concepts and all the rational knowledge, and then you get a deeper knowledge. Dionysus called it "a ray of the divine darkness encounters you." And that is where you find wisdom. So we have, as you say, to balance. You need the light; you need the mind, you need science and philosophy, theology. But then you have to go beyond them and find the dark knowledge of God, where we go beyond work and thought, and experience love, actually. See, the ultimate reality is love, and it can only be known by love, not by knowledge. As *The Cloud of Unknowing*, that wonderful treatise, said, "You can only be caught by love, and not by knowledge."

I recall seeing my first black Madonna in France and being reminded of the Hindu goddess Kali. There's the dark reflected in the goddess form, both in the Christian tradition and in the Indian tradition.

I'm so glad you said that, because that's been one of my discoveries, this black Madonna. It's so many places. I think the Madonna of Czestokowa in Poland is one, and then there's another in Spain. They're very early, about 12th century, normally, and they were more in touch with the earth, with the dark aspect of life, and so the Virgin Mary was seen not as this ethereal being, but as this very human being, and really related to the earth, to matter, to life, as every woman is. So she becomes an archetype of the humanity, of the mother, really, the mother earth, mother creation, and mother of redemption. So I think this black Madonna is very significant.

Yes, and Kali, of course, has a much more horrific image than the Christian black Madonnas.

Well, that is a problem, once you go into the darkness, into the unconscious, you meet the opposite forces. It's wonderful to open the unconscious, but there are terrible demonic forces in it, and Kali usually has a demonic aspect. Until you have to face this demonic aspect in yourself and people around you, it's a dark, violent, aggressive, and destructive force. But it's strong. And that force can't be just rejected; it has to be integrated in the deeper center. Then all that power comes into the life, into human life, and transforms it. And I think in Jesus, you see, he had this power over these demons. All these dark forces, and he was able to overcome the dark forces and integrate the power in himself instead of transcending them altogether.

I recall when I first read about Ramakrishna, the 19th-century Hindu saint, a God incarnation, and how he became enlightened through worshiping Kali. My image of Kali at that time was like a Hindu Mary or something, and then I saw the image of Kali with skulls dripping blood, snakes entwined, and so on. It just really blew me away.

Yes. And I think, like most Hindus, they accept these two opposites, you see. Shiva is the same. Shiva is the god of destruction, and he was an outcast, living in the cemeteries, and so on. And then they brought him into the pantheon, into the center, and he became a god of love. So the two aspects are held. And I think one of the things we have to learn is how to relate opposites; we'd like it to be all light, and get rid of the darkness. But in reality, the universe is light in darkness. And I always quote a wonderful theologian, St. Nicholas of Cusa. He was the Roman cardinal in the 15th century, very well respected, and he wrote a wonderful book on the vision of God, in which he speaks of the *coincidentia oppositorum,* the coincidence of opposites, light and darkness, black and white, good and evil—they all seem hopelessly apart and opposite, but when you go beyond the dualities, there is a coincidence; they come together. And that is non-duality, when the opposites come together, not simply as one that's missing the opposite, and not as two, but in a mysterious interrelationship.

It reminds me again of chaos theory, which is one of those leading-edge scientific theories that says that somewhere deep within chaos is an order. And so again, it's that relationship to the paradox, being able to live with the paradox, which is the challenge for all of us.

That's the challenge, yes. And it's very revealing, isn't it? That as you get into the depths of nature, there is this chaos, apparently. It looks like absolute chaos. I was living in India. You know what chaos there is in India. And the chaos is there. They describe Indian society as "organized chaos." The universe is largely organized chaos; there is an order, a structure, working through the chaos, but the chaos is there behind it all. And that is what Aristotle meant by "matter." First, matter is pure potentiality; it's potential for anything, and it can become good and evil and all these things, but eventually it can be integrated into the wholeness, and then the opposites come together and you find the wholeness.

Father Bede, during this conversation, we've been talking about the individual's search, and at the same time you live in an ashram, in a community. And it seems to me that if we're going to recognize the face of ourselves and others, then the future really is going to mean more community. And not just community in the large sense, but small communities, small groups of people getting together, in small circles. What do you see?

Well, that's exactly what I have in mind. I don't really believe in these large monasteries, now. On the whole, they're in decline unless we do some very great external work. It's very difficult. I believe the future is in these small communities, as you say, maybe five or six people, very often, where they can live a very simple life. The big monastery—it needs a big income to support it. But a little group of huts as we have in our ashram can be sustained quite easily, and a small community can live a simpler life and can be free from so many preoccupations with the world around and can be more deeply contemplative. So I'm hoping, actually, while I'm in America, that small communities of that kind, people coming together, sharing together, sharing their prayer together and searching for the inner center of inner peace of inner truth, of reality, begins to form. This is where I think monastic life has its future.

Father Bede, you were speaking of the future of the monastic life, and it occurs to me that so often the life of the monk is seen as separate and apart from society, and apart from the mainstream. And yet, in truth, the monk—this is a purpose of the monk, to be apart from the mainstream and at the same time reflect back to the mainstream what the mainstream doesn't have, because it's in the middle of it.

Yes, That's exactly it.

I'd like you to talk about that.

Yes. Well, that is very important. One of the ancient monks—I think it was Evagrius, a great monk of the Egyptian desert—said, "A monk is one who separates himself from all people in order to be united with all people." I think you do have to separate; you can't simply be part of the whole world order as it is. You have to separate, and then you have to reintegrate. And I always liked the ox-herd pictures in Tibetan Buddhism: You're in search of the oxen; you see his traces, and then you see the ox in the distance. You come up to it and you catch it by the tail and then you jump onto it. Then you ride off into the void and you go into the emptiness, to the darkness beyond. Then you come back to the marketplace. That for me is the goal of a monk. I belong to the Camaldolese congregation, and, interestingly enough, they have community life where you begin to learn to live with others, share with others, solitary life where you learn to be alone with God, to discover your inner self and evangelical self, where you move out to share with others. And St. Rombule, the founder of Camaldoli, at the last stage of his life, went to Hungary to spread the gospel in Hungary. They speak of the archetype of the monk—in every human being, a call to be alone, alone with God, actually. And then you've got to be able to go out of your solitude to meet people, to share and to open to the world. And that's the real hope.

There's something of value in solitude, and particularly solitude in nature. And I know that you live a very simple life, and part of it is being really connected to the land.

Yes. I think it's very important. It's difficult in America—you have a wonderful land here, but it's all very expensive [laughter]. In India, I'm sorry to say land is going up and up in value. But you still can live in extreme simplicity. And you know, you are barefoot; you feel the earth. We are just beside the river there. You are open to the whole world of nature and to the sense of the sacred in nature. And I think that's very important for a monastic life—to link with the cosmos, in a sense, in a very physical way.

Well, it may be that many of the environmental problems and challenges that we're facing today are because of that disconnection from nature, our disconnection from the earth.

I think it's so, yes. Of course, it's a difficult problem. If you don't have the technology, as in India, in many parts you have such poverty, you can't live a really full life. But once you begin with the technology, it takes over. Gandhi was trying to find a way of simple life with the necessities of life, but not with all the complications of science and technology. He was not successful. The Gandhian movement is not very vital today. But I think it has a message of how to live a really simple life in communion with nature, being aware of the earth, the trees, the water, the air, the flowers, the sun. You're living in this cosmos. In that context, to be open to other, to the world around you. And then the God within the universe is in the people and is in your own heart. The three dimensions have to come together.

EPILOGUE

Once in a great while you may be fortunate enough to meet an authentic holy person. Father Bede was such a one. He died peacefully, surrounded by friends, at his beloved ashram in south India in May 1993. In his life, he exemplified both east and west, north and south. His religion was truly universal and omuniversal, although he referred to himself as Christian. In fact, he had gone beyond any limiting definition to embrace the One in all spiritual traditions. Of course, this is our challenge as well, to transcend the apparent dichotomies and limitations, and see the underlying thread of truth, "the Tao that cannot be named," that lies at the core of every path.

Father Bede's desire to see small circles of people coming together in community to live, pray, and explore together is an idea whose time has come. No longer is it appropriate or even desirable to isolate oneself from the world and disappear to the mountaintop to meditate for years. Rather, we must integrate our spiritual practice into life, create a small circle of support, and address the challenges of our time from a grounded spiritual perspective. This is the wave of the future we can create now.

APPENDIX

RECOMMENDED READING

At the Speed of Life, by Gay and Kathlyn Hendricks

Buddha's Little Instruction Book, by Jack Kornfield

Care of the Soul, by Thomas Moore

Centering and the Art of Intimacy, by Gay and Kathlyn Hendricks

Christ in India: Essays Towards a Hindu-Christian Dialogue, by Father Bede Griffiths

Conversations with God: An Uncommon Dialogue, Book 1, by Neale Donald Walsch

Conversations with God: An Uncommon Dialogue, Book 2, by Neale Donald Walsch

The Corporate Mystic: A Guidebook for Visionaries with Their Feet Ground, by Gay Hendricks and Kate Ludeman

The Cosmic Revelation, by Father Bede Griffiths

A Deep Breath of Life: Daily Inspiration for Heart-Centered Living, by Alan Cohen

Developing a 21st-Century Mind, by Marsha Sinetar

Do What you Love, the Money Will Follow: Discovering Your Right Livelihood, by Marsha Sinetar

Elegant Choices, Healing Choices, by Marsha Sinetar

Everyday Blessings: The Inner Work of Mindful Parenting, by Jon Kabat-Zinn, Ph.D

Facing Life's Challenges: Daily Meditations for Overcoming Depression, Grief, and "The Blues," by Amy E. Dean

Full Catastrophe Living: Using the Wisdom of Your Body and Mind to Face Stress, Pain, and Illness, by Jon Kabat-Zinn, Ph.D.

Glimpse After Glimpse: Daily Reflections on Living and Dying, by Sogyal Rinpoche

The Golden String, by Father Bede Griffiths

Healing and the Mind, by Bill Moyers

Healing Words: The Power of Prayer and the Practice of Medicine, by Larry Dossey, M.D.

Learning to Love Yourself Workbook, by Gay Hendricks

Living Happily Ever After, by Marsha Sinetar

Living Dharma: Teachings of Twelve Buddhist Masters, by Jack Kornfield

The Marriage of East and West, by Father Bede Griffiths

Meaning & Medicine, by Larry Dossey, M.D.

Meditation, by Sogyal Rinpoche

Meditations to Heal Your Life, by Louise L. Hay

Ordinary People as Monks and Mystics: Livestyles for Self-Discovery, by Marsha Sinetar

A Path with Heart, by Jack Kornfield

Pocketful of Miracles, by Joan Borysenko, Ph.D.

The Power of the Mind to Heal, by Joan Borysenko, Ph.D., and Miroslav Borysenko, Ph.D.

Prayer Is Good Medicine: How to Reap the Healing Benefits of Prayer, by Larry Dossey, M.D.

Recovering the Soul: A Scientific and Spiritual Search, by Larry Dossey, M.D.

Return to the Center, by Father Bede Griffiths

Rituals of Healing: Using Imagery for Health and Wellness, by Jeanne Achterberg

A Sense of the Sacred: A Biography of Bede Griffiths, by Kathryn Spink and Father Bede Griffiths

The Tibetan Book of Living and Dying, by Sogyal Rinpoche

To Build the Life You Want, Create the Work You Love, by Marsha Sinetar

Universal Wisdom: A Journey Through the Sacred Wisdom of the World, by Father Bede Griffiths

Vedanta & Christian Faith, by Father Bede Griffiths

A Way Without Words: A Guide for Spiritually Emerging Adults, by Marsha Sinetar

Wherever You Go There You Are, by Jon Kabat-Zinn, Ph.D.

Woman as Healer, by Jeanne Achterberg

NEW DIMENSIONS
FOUNDATION

Since its inception in 1973, New Dimensions Foundation has presented lecture series, live events, and seminars; published books, sponsored educational tours, and launched a major periodical. Created to address the dramatic cultural shifts and changing human values in our society, New Dimensions has become an international forum for some of the most innovative ideas expressed on the planet. Its principal and best-known activity is New Dimensions Radio, an independent producer of radio dialogues and other programming.

During the past 20 years, many of this century's leading thinkers and social innovators have spoken through New Dimensions. The programming supports a diversity of views from many traditions and cultures. Now is a time for transformative learning and for staying open to all possibilities. We must constantly be willing to review and revise what we are creating. New Dimensions fosters the goals of living a more healthy life of mind, body, and spirit while deepening our connections to self, family, community, environment, and planet.

New Dimensions is a rare entity in the world of media—a completely independent, noncommercial radio producer. Primary support comes from listeners. Members of "Friends of New Dimensions" (FOND) are active partners in a conspiracy of hope as we celebrate the human spirit and explore new ideas, provocative insights, and creative solutions across the globe over the airwaves.

You too can play an invaluable part in this positive force for change by becoming a member of (FOND) and supporting the continued production and international distribution of New Dimensions Radio programming.

Become a Member of FOND

As a Member of "Friends of New Dimensions" (FOND), you will receive:

- *The New Dimensions Journal,* a bimonthly magazine containing captivating articles, reviews of books, video and audio tapes, current "New Dimensions" program schedules, selections of audio tapes from our archives, and much more.

- The New Dimensions Annual Tape Catalog and periodic supplements.

- A 15% discount on any product purchased through New Dimensions, including books, New Dimensions tapes and selected tapes from other producers.

- A quality thank-you gift expressing our deepest apprecition.

- The satisfaction of knowing that you are supporting the broadcast of hopeful visions to people all across the nation and the world.

Contributions are tax deductible to the extent allowed by law.

A nonprofit tax-exempt educational organization
P.O. Box 569 • Ukiah, CA 95482 • 707-468-5215
Website: www.newdimensions.org • E-mail: ndradio@igc.org

NOTES

NOTES

NOTES

NOTES

NOTES

NOTES

❧ NOTES ❧

We hope you enjoyed this Hay House/New Dimensions book. If you would like to receive a free catalog featuring additional Hay House books and products, or if you would like information about the Hay Foundation, please contact:

Hay House, Inc.
P.O. Box 5100
Carlsbad, CA 92018-5100

(800) 654-5126
(800) 650-5115 (fax)

Please visit the Hay House Website at:
www.hayhouse.com

and the New Dimensions Website at:
www.newdimensions.org